Also by Daniel Stih

Healthy Living Spaces
Top 10 Hazards Affecting Your Health

Mold Money
*How to Save Thousands of Dollars on Mold
Remediation and Make Sure the Mold is Gone*

How to Build a Healthy Home
*And Prevent the Negative Impacts on Your Health
That Can Result From Poorly Executed Green
Building Initiatives*

Unplugged
How to Find and Get Rid of EMFs in Your Home

What Your Builder Should Know
Best Practices for Building a Healthy Home

Dust Money
*How to Clean Your Home and Belongings After
Mold Remediation So You Don't Have to Throw
Everything Away*

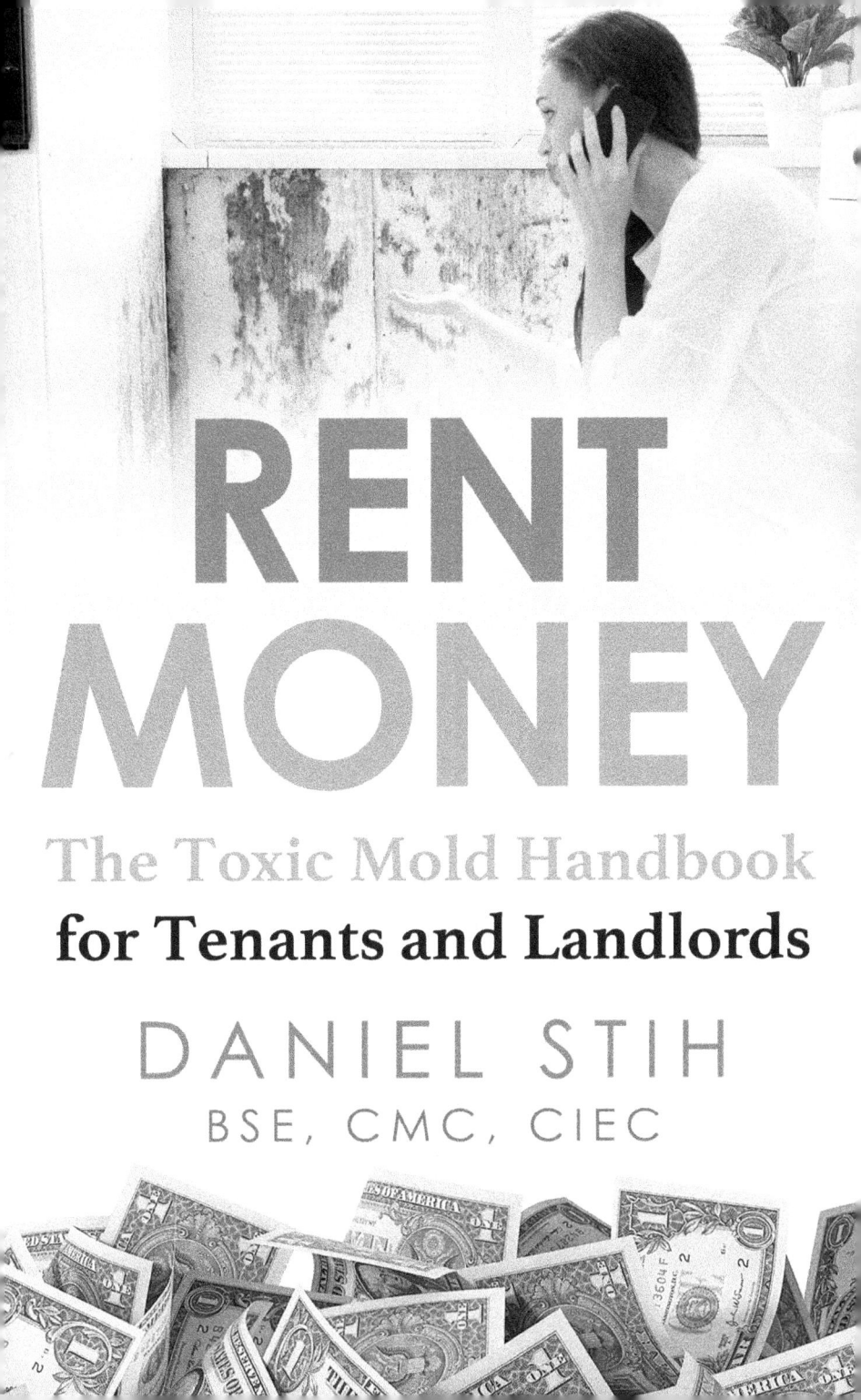

RENT MONEY

The Toxic Mold Handbook
for Tenants and Landlords

DANIEL STIH
BSE, CMC, CIEC

Disclaimer

Every building has a set of circumstances that is unique for which additional specifications or modifications of the information presented here may be required. If everything you need to know were covered, it would be a more technical read. The intent is to provide basic information that you can use to make informed decisions. If you would like specific recommendations please contact Healthy Living Spaces® to make an appointment for a consultation.

TABLE OF CONTENTS

Rights and Responsibilities

Mold Remediation

The Mold Inspection Process

Commercial Buildings

Post-remediation Verification

Cleaning After Remediation is Finished

Mold:
An Introduction

Rent Money — The Mold Handbook

Introduction

"Fungi (Molds) are more closely related to the humans that study them than to green plants which they were previously classified."

- Preface to Dictionary of the Fungi, 2008

If you're reading this book and you are a renter, you may be experiencing feelings of frustration and helplessness in regard to mold you've found in your house or apartment. It may be that your landlord had it tested and told you, "Good news! The tester said it's not a harmful mold that releases spores and it can be cleaned with a 3% hydrogen peroxide solution and then painted with a special paint. According to our maintenance department, if the mold in an area of three square feet or less, they may treat it with chemicals and paint over it per EPA Guidelines." This is incorrect.

If you are a landlord, you may worry what it is going to cost to get rid of the mold. You may wonder if you should be believe the tenants or if they are just trying to get out of their lease. Maybe you're a good person and want to do the right thing (get rid of the mold) but you're not sure what really needs to be done.

Whether you are a tenant or a landlord, you've probably tried to get advice from an expert. Unfortunately, not all so-called "experts" are created equal, and many offer unhelpful (and even harmful) advice. Everyone seems to have an opinion. Experts vary in what they say so much that it's difficult for a layperson to know what is true and what's not. My goal is to bring common sense to an issue that has become fraught with misinformation and saturated with complex jargon.

If you are a tenant, this book is going to help you understand what mold is and how it can be removed. You may think the answer is to throw your stuff away. That is not necessary. The issue is not mold that grew on them. Rather, it's what's in the dust that settled on them. The contents simply needed to be cleaned as will be explained, after the mold growth in the unit is removed.

If you are a landlord, this book is going to help you resolve a complaint in a timely manner that makes efficient use of money. It will tell you how to prevent mold, and if one of your properties has mold, under-stand why it's better to remove the mold than to try to kill or treat it.

How I Know

I've had a microscope since I was twelve, when my brothers and I opened Sun Laboratorys in the utility room of our parents' home. I let milk spoil and examined what grew under the microscope. Moving forward, I got a degree in aerospace engineering. After eleven years working for a Fortune 100 company, I quit my job, moved to a small town, and ended up working as a handyman. I had so much work that I didn't know what to do with it all. Then one day, I started to get sick and found out it was due to the hazardous stuff I was being exposed to.

I decided to find ways of testing homes and getting rid of what was making people sick. I took every class I could find on doing mold inspections, testing, and removal. My certifications are accredited by the Engineering Specialties Board (CSB).

In preparing this manuscript, I reviewed a plethora of reference materials to ensure I was not omitting any important information. One such text was *Recognition, Evaluation, and Control of Indoor Mold*. I didn't get far. Leave it to those with academic initials behind their names to explain a simple subject in a ridiculously complex manner.

The first thing I noticed was the word "recognition". What is there to recognize? If something looks or smells like mold, it's probably mold. The next thing that caught my attention is the word "evaluation".

There's nothing to evaluate. Mold is mold; that's all you need to know. You just need to get rid of it. The third word, "control", is misguided. You can prevent mold from starting to grow by preventing things from getting wet; however, you can't control mold once it has grown. Trying to control mold is not a practical action to take for reasons that will be explained. The mold simply needs to be removed, your belongings need to be dried out, and the unit needs to be repaired to prevent things from getting wet again. In layperson terms, don't water it and it can't grow. If it grows, get rid of it.I have become disenchanted with the business. What should be quite simple has become complex and costly. The mold inspection and remediation business is fraught with complex terms and bad advice. My intention is to use logic and cut to the core of the issues. By doing so, it is my hope that people can take actions that are productive in terms of locating and removing mold, while minimizing the time and money spent. This will ensure issues are resolved in a quick, practical, and cost-effective manner for all parties involved.

Mold Laws, Regulations, Guidelines, and Standards

Laws and Regulations

Most cities and states do not have mold laws. With a few exceptions, any legal language applicable to laws governing mold growing inside a building will be found in tenant-landlord laws that govern general health and safety.

In 2001, California passed the Toxic Mold Protection Act, which required regulations to be created to protect the public from toxic mold. The law required the Department of Health Services to conduct studies and consult with professionals and medical experts to determine permissible exposure limits. Due to the complexities involved with different allergens, bacteria, molds, irritants, and varying sensitiveness of individuals, it was not possible. It was also not funded. The definition of Mold in the law states "Presence of mold that exceeds the standards established by the State Department of Health Services". As a result, there could be no enforcement.

The good news is the following conditions of inadequate sanitation were added to the existing law: Dampness of habitable rooms; deteriorated, crumbling, or loose plaster; and deteriorated or ineffective waterproofing of exterior walls. It is therefore possible to require a landlord to make repairs to remediate dampness, even when mold is not visible.

In 2015, California passed a law that added to the Health and Safety Code definitions regarding substandard housing. Mold is now included in enforceable conditions in California. Visible mold growth is determined by a health or code enforcement officer, and is classified as a type of inadequate sanitation and substandard condition. The exception is minor mold found on surfaces that accumulate it, such as mold in showers. (The New York law provides a similar exception for mold on tile and grout). Tenants must notify the landlord and give them a chance to make repairs before calling to have the code enforcement team issue a citation.

Texas and Florida are two examples of states that have mold laws focusing on licensing requirements for inspectors and remediations. They do not require remediation companies to remove mold. A mold remediation company may choose to encapsulate the mold (paint over it), cover it up, or say they killed it. These laws do not require mold remediation companies to remove the mold using methods of containment to ensure the health and safety of the occupants as the mold is being removed.

Where as states such as Texas and Florida have created their own rules that licensed mold inspectors (assessors) and remediators must follow, in 2015, New Hampshire passed a law that requires professionals to be certified by a third-party, accredited, non-profit organization, such as The American Council for Accredited Certification (ACAC). Florida requires those who are licensed to pass the exam administered by the ACAC, but has their own set of rules in regard to standards and practices.

The United States Department of Housing and Urban Development (HUD), a program which provides assistance to those in low-income housing, is one of the few organizations that has regulations that clearly mention mold. HUD does not allow mold to be present, and landlords who receive money as part of the assistance program can be disqualified if mold in a unit is not removed. Unfortunately, mold has to be visible before the occupants can file a complaint. HUD inspectors are not trained on what are generally considered to be acceptable and non-acceptable methods for removing mold. An inspector cannot and will not do any testing. An inspector can only make a judgment call based on mold that is visible. An inspector may have conflicts of interest on several fronts, including pressure from landlords and supervisors to find a desired and predetermined outcome, i.e., to say there is no mold.

With a few exceptions, in states that have mold laws, the laws do not provide assistance to tenants. Municipalities do not offer free mold inspectors. If a landlord does not hire a mold inspector, then the tenant must pay for an inspection.

There are a few cities with mold laws that offer free mold inspections to enforce the law. Examples are New York City and San Diego. These cites prohibit mold in a residence and require landlords to clean it up. The inspectors will go to a property to inspect for mold if they receive a complaint. Similar to the HUD process, the inspection is limited to visible and obvious mold. There is no money allocated for sending samples of visible mold to a laboratory, collecting air samples, or testing for hidden mold. If the inspector doesn't see mold, they will simply will say there is no mold. In cities where the code does not explicitly prohibit it, if the inspector notes the presence of mold, a landlord could paint over the mold, in which case the city inspector won't see it on a follow-up inspection and consider it effectively remediated. In that case, the tenant must hire their own inspector to test for mold hidden in wall cavities and then take the landlord to court to enforce having the mold removed properly.

In 2018, the City of New York passed local law No. 55, Control of Pests and Other Asthma Allergen Triggers, which makes visible mold a violation. Unfortunately, the presence of mold in an amount measuring a total less than ten square feet is considered a non-hazardous violation. Given that typically most of the mold present in a given space is hidden, this definition does little to help tenants. The good news is that a non-hazardous condition constitutes a hazardous one if the mold condition that was the cause of the non-hazardous violation continues to be present. In other words, if the mold is painted over and the mold inspector does a WallChek®, and there is still mold present, one can argue the non-hazardous condition has continued to be present past the time period allowed for corrections, in which case the presence of the mold inside the walls becomes a hazardous violation, even though less than ten square feet of mold is visible. Note: There is no study regarding how many square feet of mold is required for mold to be a health hazard. The ten square foot rule was established arbitrarily by New York City when they published the first edition on guidelines for mold remediation in 2002. The EPA subsequently copied New York's guidelines. The misconception that there is a relationship between health effects and a measurable amount of mold continues to be propagated in sources that reference the New York guidelines from 2002.

The general recommendation of most public heath organizations regarding mold is to remove the mold, and not to say a space is habitable or not based on testing. This is because of the variability inherent in air sampling, detection limits, dilution with outdoor air, and other factors. A single air test (or even a few) may not detect mold growth inside of a building. The text *Bioaerosols: Assessment and Control* states that the ultimate method of assessing the effectiveness of a mold remediation project is the ability of the occupants to inhabit the space after remediation without a reaction. The occupants, not air samples or other means of testing, are the measure of the effectiveness of a remediation project.

If an inspector collects air samples, the inspector should not just send the lab report to the parties involved. They should put in writing two important things: first that there is no mold in the building (something they would never do), and second that there is no way an occupant could be affected by bacteria or any other irritants due to the same moisture that led the mold to grow.

Guidelines

The first public document published on mold remediation was *Guidelines on Assessment and Remediation of Fungi in Indoor Environments* by the New York City Department of Health. The guidelines in this document are good with the exception that they differ depending on how many square feet of mold is visible. Depending on whether there is one, ten, or 100 square feet of visible mold, the guidelines range from

stating the homeowner can do it themselves to rec-
ommending they hire a professional remediation company. The intention was to provide free and practical
advice. But there's no way of knowing how much
mold is present until you cut the wall open. Most of
the time, most of the mold is not visible until walls are
cut open. Most mold remediators would be out of a job
if they based their estimates on the amount of visible
mold. Yet many, and some insurance companies, continue to use this guideline to determine what needs to
be done and how. The good thing is the most recent
edition says to use soap and water, not bleach. Another
good thing is that the document is free and can be
down-loaded off the internet.

A short time after New York published their guidelines, the United States Environmental Protection
Agency (EPA) published *Mold Remediation in Schools
and Commercial Buildings* (2001) and *A Brief Guide to
Mold, Moisture and Your Home* (2002). I don't reference
the EPA guidelines because they were copied, verbatim
from what New York had written, and while New York
has updated their guidelines (2008), the EPA has not. In
recent years, some states, including Florida, have
copied the EPA's guidelines, which are in turn a copy
of New York's initial (arbitrary) guidelines.

Want to learn more

Download a free copy of the 2008 version of *Guidelines on Assessment and Remediation of Fungi in Indoor Environments*, by the New York City Department of Health, https://www1.nyc.gov/assets/doh/downloads/pdf/epi/epi-mold-guidelines.pdf

Standards

The only standard for mold remediation is the ANSI/IICRC S520 *Standard for Professional Mold Remediation* by the Institute of Inspection, Cleaning and Restoration Certification (IICRC). This document was put through an intense review by the American National Standards Institute (ANSI) which considered (and responded to) every comment made by the general public. It is the standard every professional mold remediator and inspector says they follow. The document costs $125; there are no free or preview copies online.

Want to learn more?

The Institute of Inspection, Cleaning and Restoration (IICRC) has a companion document, the *S520 Reference Guide for Professional Mold Remediation*, which explains the rational behind what's written in the *S520 Standard for Professional Mold Remediation*.

Laws, Guidelines & Standards

....

Guidelines on Assessment and Remediation of Fungi in Indoor Environments. New York City Department of Health, April 2002, 2008.

Mold Remediation in Schools and Commercial Buildings. The United States Environmental Protection Agency (EPA), 2001.

A Brief Guide to Mold, Moisture and Your Home. The United States Environmental Protection Agency (EPA), 2002.

"LOCAL LAWS OF THE CITY OF NEW YORK FOR THE YEAR 2018, No. 55."

Rent Money — The Mold Handbook

Introduction to Mycology

MYTH: *Mold is everywhere. Microscopic mold spores exist naturally almost everywhere, which makes the concept of true "removal" impossible.*

FACT: Mold growth does not exist everywhere and should not exist indoors. The *S520 Standard for Professional Mold Remediation* contains definitions regarding what is considered actual mold growth.

What Mold Is

The following section is meant to provide an understanding of what mold is and why it should be removed, not treated. Do you wash your hands after going to the bathroom? What about before you eat dinner? Why bother if bacteria are everywhere? It's common sense. It's also common sense that mold should not be growing inside a building — it doesn't matter where or what kind. You wash, not treat, your hands to remove bad stuff, and so it should be with mold growth. You need to remove the growth, not treat the building.

A fungus (mold) is an organism that is devoid of chlorophyll, obtains its nutrients by absorption, and reproduces by spores. Organisms studied by mycologists are mostly placed in the kingdom Fungi. Some molds, however, belong in other kingdoms. If we were to consider all of the 1-1.5 million species of mold mycologists say exists, the species would be placed in three to five different kingdoms. This is because there are two generally accepted systems biologists use to classify life.

One way to organize life is based on evolution. In this hierarchical system, organisms are grouped on their relationship to an ancestor and its decedents. The group an organism is placed in is based on DNA. The other way of classifying is grouping organisms based on characteristics. For molds, characteristics include morphology, nutritional modes, and ecology. In this system, all organisms that have the characteristics of mold would be classified as fungi.

The problem with grouping all molds into the kingdom of fungi is the DNA of all molds cannot be traced to a single ancestor. An analogy would be if some humans originated from bacteria, others from plants, and others from primates, then choosing a single group to place humans in would not be possible. The DNA of all humans is similar enough to place them in the same group, but it's not so for all of the organisms that behave and look like mold.

Introduction to Mycology

Mildew, although technically a type of fungi, is not what is commonly called mold. Mildew is a plant disease. Powdery mildew is caused Erysiphaceae; downy mildew by Peronosporaceae species.

Unlike the fragile cell walls of bacteria, mold spores are made of chitin, one of the hardest substances known to man (the same as found in skeletons). This enables a spore to survive dry conditions and freezing temperatures. It protects it from heat, chemicals, and disinfectants.

Spores are not required for mold to reproduce. A minute fragment from almost any part of the organism is able to produce a new growing point and start a new individual. Insects, dust mites, and amoeba digest spores and fragments of mold. Their droppings may supply what's required for mold growth. The roots of mold, hyphae, may be enough for mold to start growing when there is adequate moisture.

What Mold Needs to Grow

Water is the most important requirement. Don't water it and mold cannot grow. Just as plants, trees, and flowers have different moisture preferences, different types of mold prefer different amounts of water. Some

17

require materials to be soaking wet. These include *Stachybotrys* and *Fusarium*. Some prefer materials to be saturated, but not soaking. These include *Alternaria, Ulocladium, Cladosporium,* and *Aspergillus.* You might suspect molds have methods for conserving water as needed for survival. Some species product mannitol and other compounds for osmotic regulation.

Food. You are what you eat, which is also the case for mold. What substrates a species can use as food is governed by what digestive enzymes it is capable of producing and releasing. The types of mold that grow indoors prefer cellulose-based materials. Examples are the paper backing on drywall (wall board), carpet, paper, and wood. House dust contains microscopic bits of skin, sawdust, and other organic debris that can support mold growth. When you see mold growing around the edges of a glass window in the winter, that mold is growing on the surface dust.

Time. Mold needs time to grow. Some experts say mold can grow within 24-72 hours of a material becoming wet. What they mean is "visible" growth. A spore can start growing immediately after it gets wet. You may not see a sporulating colony for 72 hours or more.

Just as different plants and flowers have different time requirements, different molds need different amounts of moisture for longer or shorter periods of time before they sporulate. Some types become visible to the naked eye in approximately two to three days; for others it may be a week to ten days before growth is visible.

What Mold Does Not Need to Grow

Temperature is not a factor. Most molds prefer temperatures between 70° and 90° F. Mold can, however, germinate between approximately 32° F (freezing) and 120° F. Consider that if you leave food in a refrigerator long enough, mold will grow on it. Molds such as yeast prefer cooler conditions. I once thought mold was not capable of growing at temperatures below freezing because once water freezes, there is no longer a source of moisture available. In fact, there are cold-loving species of mold which are capable of growing below freezing. Mold is capable of growing at temperatures higher than 90° F but they are inhibited by competing bacteria and other organisms which prefer the higher temperatures.

Air is not required for mold growth. Although it's true that most molds require oxygen gas, they do not require air. They need oxygen to complete their metabolism but can grow with as little as 0.5 % oxygen gas. Some molds can grow in either the presence or absence of oxygen and adjust their metabolic process accordingly. *Salmonella, E. coli,* and yeast are examples of organisms that grow better with oxygen but do not require it. This is why pasteurization was invented. Canning food under a vacuum to get rid of oxygen (air) will not prevent mold from growing. Food manufacturers know this, so they displace oxygen in packages instead by pumping carbon dioxide, nitrogen, hydrogen, or another inert gas into the package — a process called modified atmosphere packaging. For some foods, a combination of processes are used: food may be heated (pasteurized) and then placed under a vacuum.

Light is not a factor for growing mold. It's a myth that mold prefers to grow in the dark. Dark places are simply more likely to be wet and stay damp longer than places exposed to direct sunlight. Mold can grow in the dark or the light. Some molds prefer alternating states of light and dark to initiate sporulation.

How Mold Spreads

Mold spreads as its source of moisture spreads. Mold can only grow where it is wet. If the wet area is limited to a small spot, mold cannot grow outside of it. If the source of water is not stopped, and water wicks up a wall or drips into a space below (from the second story), mold will spread to those areas.

Imagine a field of dirt. If you were to only water a spot in the middle, weeds and grass would only grow in that spot. The rest of the field would remain barren. But if you flood the field, a lot of plants are going to spout up before it dries.

Mold growth starts with a spore. Like a seed, the spore grows roots and then branches.

It may be said that as soon as something becomes wet, there is mold growth — a germ tube. A spore begins to grow by forming a germ tube, the tip of which expands to form a network of hyphae (roots) called mycelium. During its initial growth, a spore can sustain itself without food, just like how a seed for a tree contains adequate nutrients to support germination. The process begins as soon as the spore gets wet. It's a numbers game. The reason Mother Nature produces so many spores (similar to how many pollen spores are produced by plants and trees) is that most spores will not stay wet long enough or have a sufficient food source to survive past germination.

Mold has a number of creative ways to reproduce which are influenced by the environmental conditions and the spore's state. The technical terms are: sexual, asexual, and parasexual reproduction. The normal way a mold reproduces is asexual reproduction: it has sex with itself. The mold replicates itself. This is done by producing spores. The offspring are genetically identical to the parent. When conditions are optimal (wet) a mold will grow and produce spores.

As conditions become less favorable (when the environment begins to dry or the mold feels threatened by competing organisms), a mold may use sexual reproduction to mate with another of its kind. To mate, molds fuse their hyphae (roots) into one interconnected network. Genetic material is passed through the hyphae (roots), after which a sac is formed. The sac protects the offspring spores until conditions become favorable.

It has been said that the single most important challenge faced by mold is an encounter with another of the same species. Fungi have a set of genes controlling hyphal fusion. Incompatible stains are capable of mating. In the event the union is deemed a mistake, molds have a function that resists the transfer of cytoplasmic components and nuclei during the growth phase, essentially initiating a lethal killing of the cells.

To summarize, the only mandatory requirement for mold growth is moisture. If you want to prevent mold from growing, keep things dry. When an accident happens and things get wet, dry things out as quick as possible.

Points to Remember

- The *ANSI/IICRC S520 Standard for Professional Mold Remediation* by the Institute of Inspection, Cleaning and Restoration Certification (IICRC) is the standard for mold remediation. If you have questions, reference it.

- The only thing mold needs to start growing is

water, i.e., wet or damp building materials. Get a moisture meter and use it to check how damp a materials is. For wood and drywall, less than 15% moisture is considered dry, 17-19% is damp, and 20% or greater is wet. If your readings suggest a material is damp, take immediate action to identify the source and stop it. Dry the materials that are wet.

....

Introductory Mycology. C.J. Alexopoulos, C.W. Mims, and M. Blackwell. John Wiley & Sons, Inc., 1996.

Food and Indoor Fungi. Second Edition. Robert A. Samson, J. Houbraken, U. Thrane, J.C. Frisvad, and B. Andersen. Westerdijk Fungal Biodiversity Institute, 2019.

"Can molds grow in the absence of air?" Edward Richter, Faculty, Food Microbiology, Ohio State University, http://www.madsci.org/posts/archives/2000-01/948506647.Mi.r.html, Jan, 2000.

Ainsworth & Bisby's Dictionary of the Fungi. 10th Edition. Edited by Paul M. Kirk, Paul F. Cannon, David W. Minter, and Joost A. Stalpers. CAB International, 2008.

Introduction to Mycology: Mold in Buildings. John Haines, et. al, The McCrone Institute, 2008.

The Chemistry of Fungi. James R Hanson. The Royal Society of Chemistry, 2008.

Health Effects

Myth: *Not all mold is harmful.* Fact: All molds are capable of eliciting a physical response.

Much of the disputes between tenants and landlords are the result of opinions and beliefs based on misinformation. Disputes are often resolved once the parties involved clear their heads. Those who know the truth can skip ahead to the section on preventing mold. Consider skipping ahead if you agree with all of the following:

- It doesn't matter what kind of mold is present.

- It doesn't matter if mold growth is dead, alive, dormant, or active.

- Bleach does not kill mold.

- Mold is not the only organism that grows in damp environments. Mold, therefore, is not required for occupants in a damp building to have symptoms.

- It is futile, counterproductive, and a waste of

money (not to mention it can create new problems) to try and kill mold and other organisms that thrive in wet environments.

- The only way to remove mold (and these other organisms) is to remove or restore the affected building materials. Dry the area, remove porous materials, then wire brush and clean what remains.

It may seem there is a lack of clarity about the degree to which mold is harmful, what type of harm it might do, and what symptoms a person might experience. This is because there is a lot we don't know, and there can be synergistic effects depending on an individual's health state. One thing is for sure: none of this stuff is good for you. It's not worth gambling with your health by risking unnecessary exposure.

Most Molds Are Not Pathogenic

This is generally true for the symptoms associated with the types of mold that grow indoors when building materials get wet. That does not mean these molds do not cause health symptoms. Pathogenic means an organism causes a disease by growing inside your body. Most symptoms associated with damp indoor environments are not due to mold growing in the body, rather to the exposure to dead organisms, particles, and chemicals these organisms produce as part of their normal metabolisms.

Common Mold Symptoms

According to the New York City Department of Health guidelines on mold remediation, the most common symptoms associated with mold are allergic reactions, runny nose, sneezing, postnasal drip with sore throat, eye irritation, coughing, wheezing, and aggravation of asthma. Other symptoms might include cold and flu-like symptoms, a dry hacking cough or sore throat, headaches, and nausea.

According to *Damp Indoor Spaces and Health*, a committee that reviewed available literature determined there is sufficient evidence to conclude an association with exposure to damp environments and upper respiratory (nasal and throat) tract symptoms, coughing, wheezing, and asthma symptoms in asthmatic individuals, with or without the presence of mold.

Inhalation is a primary pathway for exposure. Once settled on surfaces, mold spores and particles associated with growth are resuspended by disturbances such as walking, cleaning, opening curtains or blinds, and plopping down on furniture.

Dermal contact is a significant pathway for exposure. The chemical metabolites that molds produce as they secrete enzymes to break down food can pass though skin and cause rashes, irritation, and nose-bleeds.

Size May Matter

The percentage of spores deposited in the respiratory tract is a function of size. The smaller a spore, the greater the chance it will be deposited in the lungs. Small spores such as *Aspergillus* and *Penicillium*, have a greater chance of depositing in the lungs. *Stachybotrys* (what the media coined "toxic and black mold") is a relatively large spore. The spores of *Cladosporium*, a common outdoor mold, can be small or large depending on the species. The species found indoors is small. Although *Cladosporium* might be considered a less toxic mold, there is therefore, the potential to breathe more of these spores compared to those of larger types.

It's More than Mold

According to *Damp Indoor Spaces and Health*, mold is not required for occupants in a damp building to have symptoms. If mold is not required, what else might be a factor in the association between the presence of water damage and health symptoms? The following might also be present:

Endotoxins (Gram-negative Bacteria)
Endotoxins are found in the cell walls of a class of bacteria known as gram-negative. Gram-negative bacteria thrive in damp and water-damaged buildings. As they dry, the bacteria desiccate into fragments that become airborne. Exposure is through the air from the dead bacteria.

Actinomycetes (Gram-positive Bacteria)
Actinomycetes are a type of bacteria that form long, branching cell chains that mimic mold and form spores that are released into the air. Actinomycetes are commonly found in soil. They produce compounds responsible for earthy, musty, odors, and are a known agent of hypersensitivity pneumonitis, also known as farmer's lung disease.

Amoebae (Protozoa)
In one study, amoebae were detected in 22% of 124 samples collected from materials with water damage. Amoebae act synergistically with certain bacteria and may engulf bacteria while feeding. The engulfed bacteria remain alive and infectious. An example is Legionella, a bacteria associated with illness in commercial buildings with cooling towers.

A similar synergy is found in lichen, which is composed of an algae and a fungus. The algae provides the fungus with carbohydrates and the fungus provides the algae with protection from the elements.

MVOCS and VOCS

The 2001 California mold law defines the "identification" (of mold) to mean, "The process of recognizing mold, water damage, or microbial volatile organic compounds (MVOCS) in indoor environments." MVOCs are responsible for the odors associated with mold, bacteria, and damp conditions. Mold may be present without a musty odor. There may not be an odor if conditions are dry because the source of moisture was fixed.

When building materials get wet, they emit odors called volatile organic compounds (VOCs). Unless the material is removed, the odor may never completely go away. VOCs are too numerous to list. Laboratories can't even identify all of them.

Mycotoxins

Mycotoxins are secondary metabolites and not required for mold to grow. A mold may produce mycotoxins when its survival is threatened by competing molds, bacteria, or other organisms. The presence of a potentially toxigenic species does not mean mycotoxins are present.

When produced, a mold slathers itself with the toxins. It is not just spores that contain the toxin; all of the structure — roots, stalks, and spores — is coated. Mycotoxins are not gases. They are large molecules that do not readily off-gas. They attach to particles. An analogy is how chemicals in diesel exhaust attach to soot particles, and how chemicals in pesticides attach to dust particles on the floor so the chemicals remain for some time after they are applied.

Most poisonings from mold are not from living in moldy buildings, rather from eating moldy food. Ergotism, the oldest known mold disease, was caused by *Claviceps purpurea*. It caused mass poisonings in the Middle Ages known as St. Anthony's Fire. Stachybotrystoxicosis, a disease caused by the ingestion of food contaminated with *Stachybotrys*, was responsible for the deaths of horses in Russia in the 1930s. Aflatoxins came to attention in London in 1960, when thousands of turkeys and ducks died. An investigation found the feed mill was contaminated with moldy nuts from Brazil contaminated with *Aspergillus* type mold. When people say they are allergic to nuts, they may actually be allergic to mold.

Other Irritants

Water damage is associated with the peptidoglycans in the cell walls of gram-positive bacteria, insects, allergens and irritants associated with insects, and glucans in the air that originate from the cell walls of molds. It's impractical to evaluate a building and its occupants for exposure to all of these. The general recommendation in *Damp Indoor Spaces and Health* is to remove water damaged materials vs. attempting to quantify the significance of water damage in relation to health effects, exposure risk, and the absence or presence of mold.

Is it Safe?

According to the New York City Health Department Guidelines, several factors influence the likelihood an individual might experience health effects following exposure to mold. These include the nature of the fungal material (allergenic, toxic, irritant, infectious), degree of exposure, and susceptibility of individuals. Susceptibility varies with genetic predisposition (age, state of health, concurrent exposures) and previous sensitization. Because of the variation of individual susceptibility and the lack of reliable biological markers, it is not possible to determine a safe or unsafe level of exposure to mold.

Want to learn more?

The best text on health effects from mold and the presence of water damage is *Damp Indoor Spaces and Health*. A free copy can be downloaded on the website for the National Academies of Sciences, Engineering, and Medicine at www.nap.edu/catalog/11011/damp-indoor-spaces-and-health.

Points to Remember

- If you came away with no clear answer regarding what you can expect in regard to health effects if you find a certain type of mold in your living space, that's because there is no clear answer. Prudent avoidance is suggested. If there is mold, remediation is advised, regardless of what kind of mold is detected. Remediation of water damage is suggested even if mold is not present.

- Treating and killing mold is not the answer to resolving a complaint regarding the presence of mold, moisture, or odors. As complex as the issue might seem, the solution is simple: to prevent mold, keep things dry; to get rid of mold, cut out the moldy materials and clean up the rest of the mess with a wire brush and soap and water.

- If you test and do not find mold, the symptoms occupants may be experiencing could be from other things associated with dampness and moisture. The remediation protocol is the same: identify and repair the source of moisture, remove porous materials that got wet, and clean up the mess with a wire brush and soap and water. Applying a sanitizer or antimicrobial will not help.

- Health risk depends on the individual. If you think your health is being compromised by the presence of water damage or mold, ask your doctor. It is prudent to remove mold as soon as possible, in a proper way, with proper containment.

Guidance for Clinicians on the Recognition and Management of Health Effects Related to Mold Exposure and Moisture Indoors. Story, Eileen, et. al, The University of Connecticut Health Center, 2005.

"Endotoxins." Chin S. Yang, Ph.D., EMLab P&K, 2003.

www.emlab.com/media/resources/Endotoxins.pdf. "Amoebae and other protozoa in material samples from moisture-damaged buildings." Yli-Pirilä T, et al., *Environmental Research.* 2004 Nov;96(3):250-6.

"Effects of Airflow and Changing Humidity on the Aerosolization of Respirable Fungal Fragments and Conidia of Botrytis cinerea." Anne Mette Madsen, *Applied and Environmental Microbiology.*

"Adverse Human Health Effects Associated with Molds in the Indoor Environment." American College of Occupational and Environmental Medicine, 2011.

Asthma in the Workplace. Jean-Luc Malo, et al., CRC Press, 2013.

Biological pollutants in indoor air. Sonja S. Radakovi, et al. Vojnosanit Pregl. 2014.

Health Effects

Mold in Housing: Information for First Nations Communities—Housing Managers' Guide. Canada Mortgage and Housing Corporation (CMHC), 2011.

"Colonization of Candida: prevalence among tongue-pierced and non-pierced immunocompetent adults." Zadik Yehuda, Burnstein Saar, Derazne Estella, Sandler Vadim, Ianculovici Clariel, Halperin Tamar. March, 2010. *Oral Diseases.* 16 (2): 172–5.

4th Edition, Medically Important Fungi, A Guide to Identification. Davise H. Larone, ASM Press, Washington, D.C., 2002.

"Microbial volatile organic compounds in the air of moldy and mold-free indoor environments." *Indoor Air.* 2008 Apr;18(2):113-24, Schleibinger H., Laussmann D., Bornehag C.G., Eis D., Rueden H.

Rent Money — The Mold Handbook

How to Prevent Mold

If you can prevent mold from growing, you can skip much of this book. Preventing moisture problems will prevent mold from growing. The following section details ways moisture problems are created and how to prevent them.

How to Prevent Mold

General Tips

Accidents Happen

When there is a leak, do whatever it takes to dry things fast. If carpet gets wet, remove it. If wall board (drywall) gets wet and it's not dry (as indicated by a reading of less than 17% using the pins on the moisture meter) within three days, cut the drywall out on the third day. Don't wait for the forth, when mold may begin to be visible. Done sooner, it's a handyman job. Done later, it's a mold remediator's job.

Want to learn more?

See *The ANSI/IICRC S500 Standard and Reference Guide for Professional Water Damage Restoration* provides standards and practical principles for drying and water damage restoration.

Suggestions for Landlords to Prevent Mold Growth

Before You Rent It

Do a mold inspection and fix any problems that are identified before signing a lease with a new tenant. Look for leaks or signs of water damage in the following places:

- Under kitchen sinks

- Behind the washing machine

- Around and behind the hot water heater

- The walls around and behind toilets

Consider making improvements, such as:

- If the freezer has an ice maker, shut off, disconnect, cap, and seal the water hose.

- Do not have window-mounted air conditioners. They are not weathertight. If you have one, protect it with a canopy over the window. Seal the space between the unit and window opening with caulk.

- Install splash guards on the edges of bathtubs so water cannot leak out if the shower curtain is not pulled tight.

- If the bathroom does not have one, install a fan.

- Install a motion sensor in the switch on the wall for the fan so that the fan automatically turns on when someone is in the bathroom.

- Inspect the exhaust duct behind the dryer. Check to make sure it is not kinked or loose, and that it is vented to the outside. It should not exhaust air into an attic or crawlspace.

- Do not have gas space heaters that don't need to be vented because they are 100% efficient. They emit large amounts of water vapor.

- Install a whole-house water shutoff valve. These shut the water off when something happens like a pipe freezing or a hose bursting at a washing machine or toilet.

- If you are remodeling, consider installing one-piece, plastic showers, as they can't leak.

- Walk around the house and make sure water can't

collect next to it from gutters or the slope of the land, especially if there is a basement or crawl-space.

- Make sure you calk around all four sides of doors and windows (including the top), using a ladder if necessary.

Inspect the Crawlspace

Crawlspaces are places where water from plumbing leaks and rain and snow that collects next to the house can easily infiltrate, which can cause moisture and mold problems. If there is a crawlspace, put on a res-pirator and disposable suit and go into the crawlspace to check for the following:

- Look on the ground for evidence of plumbing leaks. If you find one, repair it immediately and clean any soil that got wet.

- Check along the perimeter of the foundation for evidence of water leaking in. If you find evidence of a water leak, make modifications to divert water from the foundation.

- Remove any carpet, wood, or cardboard laying on the ground. These trap moisture and are sources of food for mold. Don't let the tenant store stuff in the crawlspace.

How to Prevent Mold

- If there is mold on floor joists or the bottom of the subfloor, it may because the wood was installed damp or moldy when the structure was built. Perception is king. Use a wire-brush to clean it off. The same goes for the wood framing in an attic.

- Do not install a vapor barrier (plastic) on the ground in a crawlspace. These do not work unless the seams are glued to make the finished job water and airtight. Unless the barrier is airtight, moisture and mold that builds up under the plastic will escape into the air and infiltrate the occupied space. Instead of improving conditions, you will have created a problem. If you install a vapor barrier, use the same materials used to install vapor barriers under concrete slabs when a commercial structure is built. Secure it up to the rim joist and make it airtight.

Ventilate the Crawlspace

One of the most effective ways to keep crawlspaces dry and to prevent air in the crawlspace from rising up into the living space, is to install power vents. All crawlspaces should be power-ventilated. In places where there are vents to the crawlspace, install fans (power-vents) that blow outward. Don't set the fans/ventilators on humidity controls or timers. Run them all the time. After installing the power vents, seal any vents that do not have power exhaust fans, as there needs to be suction.

Ventilation should exchange air in the crawlspace four times every hour, or once every 15 minutes. If you're not good at math, assume you need two vents per 1,000 square feet of living space. For those who do math, multiply the square footage of the crawlspace (living space above it) by the height of the crawlspace. This is the cubic feet. Divide that by 15 to determine the CFM (cubic feet per minute) of fan power needed.

For example: a 40 foot long x 40 foot wide x 2 feet high crawlspace is 3200 cubic feet. Dividing 3200 by 15 equals 213, the CFM of air flow needed. If a fan vent is rated at a maximum of 110 CFM, two units would be required. The fans should be installed on opposite ends of the crawlspace. Unused vents, those where power vents are not installed, should be sealed. Makeup air will come from leaks in the flooring and foundation. If done effectively, this creates a lower air pressure in the crawlspace relative to the living space, and keeps odors and contaminates out of the living space.

Perform a Check-Up Every 6 Months

Like checking the fluids when you change the oil in your car, periodically check for leaks and water damage. Every six months, ask the tenant to allow you to enter to check for water damage and leaks. Schedule this soon after there has been a heavy rain. Purchase a moisture meter and take it with you. During your inspection, do the following:

- Check under the kitchen sink for leaks.

- Check behind the washing machine for leaks.

- Check the tiles in showers and around tubs for cracks and missing grout and make repairs as needed.

- Check behind toilets for leaks.

- If there is a crawlspace, go inside it and check for leaks and dampness.

- Using the pins on the moisture meter, check the walls under the corners of windows, next to exterior doors, and ceilings. Check areas you suspect there is the potential for a leak. For wood and drywall, readings less than 15% are considered dry, 17-19% is considered damp, and 20% or greater is wet. If something has been wet for some time (say, a week) mold may have started to grow. Investigate and make repairs immediately and consider testing for mold.

Suggestions for Tenants to Prevent Mold Growth

If your landlord has read the first section of this book and given you a nice, dry place to live that's free of mold, keep it that way. Take care of the place.

Notify your landlord if you notice even the smallest of leaks. When there is a leak, things need to be dried out fast. The clock is ticking. You might not think a leak is serious enough, or that you're prepared enough to have the landlord visit. Mold takes only few days to grow. Leaks need to be repaired and actions taken to dry things out as soon as possible.

If you notice shower or tile grout missing, let the landlord know repairs are needed. If you have kids that splash in the tub, ask for tub guards. These have a peel and stick backing and are placed on the tub where the tub meets the wall. They prevent water from leaking out around the shower curtain. Also, always turn the bathroom fan on when showering and the kitchen fan on when cooking.

How to Prevent Mold

Cold Weather Tips

Regardless of how dry it might seem, when something gets cold enough, moisture will condense on it. When it get cold enough, windows start sweating and water begins condensing inside walls and in places you can't see. To prevent mold from growing, it's imperative to prevent moisture from condensing. There are two ways to do this. The first is to reduce the level of relative humidity, the other is to increase the temperature of surfaces. There are challenges to each. The following are a few things you can do to help:

- Use an electric space heater if it gets too cold.

- Don't place a couch or bed in contact with an exterior wall. Leave a few inches behind it so warm air can reach the walls. Otherwise you may find mold on the back of your couch and the wall behind it. Mold can begin growing in winter and it might be spring or summer before you discover it. By that time, the mold will be dry, and you may be wondering why it grew in the first place.

- Don't close the doors to bedroom closets. There needs to be ventilation inside closets to keep the walls inside closets warm. If the door to a closet is closed, mold can grow on your stuff, and on walls inside the closet. This happens because when the door is closed, the closet isn't heated. It gets

47

colder and colder and eventually microscopic bits of moisture condense on the cold walls. Condensation occurs first on the coldest surfaces. This may be inside a closet on an exterior, north-facing wall, under carpet, on contents that are stuffed against an outside wall, or inside bags and storage boxes where there is little ventilation and it get very cold.

- Never put a mattress or futon on the floor in direct contact with the ground. There needs to be a space between the ground for ventilation, other-wise moisture from the ground gets trapped and you may find mold on the bottom of your futon or mattress.

- Don't run a humidifier in the winter. If a room is small enough, and the temperature cold enough, condensation will occur, and mold will grow on exterior walls, inside closets, and on windows.

- Pets exhaust just as much moisture in their breath as humans. The more pets you have, the more moisture there will be indoors. When there is enough moisture, condensation occurs. When it is really cold, or if you have lots of pets or several people occupying a space, take steps to exhaust excess moisture outside. Turn on the bathroom fans and leave the doors open to the bathrooms so air came be pulled from the living space, into the bathrooms, and exhausted outside. Run the fans all the time.

- Don't turn the heat down to save money. Keep the heat set to normal. The cooler it gets, the easier it will be for condensation to occur. If you have a bedroom or an office room you are using as storage or don't use much, you may be tempted to keep the door to it closed and turn the heat down in those rooms. Don't. Keep all the rooms conditioned (heated and air conditioned if there is A/C) year round.

How to Handle a Mold Discovery

How to Handle a Mold Discovery

What a Landlord Should/Should Not Do and Say

What to Do if a Tenant Says They See Mold

Go and look. Ask the tenant to show you what they think is mold. If it looks like mold, it probably is, and there is no need to test it. Skip to remediation.

If you aren't sure if what the tenant thinks is mold, is actually mold, then test it. You can do this yourself. Ask the tenant to be present so they are satisfied you collected samples from the most suspicious places. That way, if test results come back negative, the tenant can not argue you didn't test all of the areas they think are mold. Use the tape lift method. (See the chapter on testing.)

If there's no source of water nearby, then what you're sampling may not be mold. It could be candle soot, dirt, a smudge, magic marker, a washing machine hose rubbing on a wall, or a lot of other things. If it's not "mold growth" the mold lab will not be able to tell what the substance is. They will be clear on whether it is or is not mold growth.

What *Not* to Do if a Tenant Says They See Mold

Don't say, "I'll have my handyman look at it." Handymen are not mold inspectors and not trained to perform mold remediation. The exception is if a tenant tells you there is an active leak. That can be a difficult situation, as the leak needs to be repaired immediately, but if mold has already grown, care must be taken not to disturb the mold. Ask the tenants if there is a leak. If there is not an active leak, you don't need a handyman. You may need a mold inspector or a mold remediator.

If there is an active leak, you are in a conundrum. Fans are normally used to expedite drying so that mold goes not grow, but if mold has had time to grow, using a fan to dry things will blow mold and dust around as repairs as being performed and contaminate the occupant's belongings. Care must be taken as repairs as being done to protect belongings (contents) and the living space from what is defined as "cross-contamination." To contain the mold, you will need a professional mold remediation company. The remediation company will set up an air scrubber such that a negative air pressure is created in the work area. This needs to be done before cutting into walls. This may be a scenario in which to consider giving the tenant their deposit back and allowing them to move out. You may not know for certain there is not mold until you cut into a wall to make repairs — at which point, if you don't have containment set up the tenant may claim you contaminated their belongings.

If you have a leak and things are wet, call your insurance company. Use the keywords "leak," "water damage," "sudden," and "unexpected."

What to Do if a Tenant Says they Smell Mold

The odor may or may not be from mold. It could be from moisture and damp conditions that have not led to mold growth. Bacteria and other microorganisms produce musty odors. Alternatively, the odor could be sewer gas, a dead animal, or a gas leak.

Use a moisture meter to check the walls and floor in the area the tenant says they smell mold. If you find a damp area and it smells like mold, there probably is mold. If conditions are dry, testing for mold might be helpful. Testing can eliminate mold as a possible cause of the odor if the results are negative. If the test results are negative and things are dry, it might be concluded the odor is not due to mold or dampness.

To determine if it's mold causing the odor, you need a mold inspector who knows how to collect samples from wall cavities using a method called the WallChek®. A WallChek® is a small, quarter-inch tube that is inserted into a wall. A vacuum pump is used to pull air out of the wall. The sample is then sent to a laboratory. If mold is detected, it might be better to let the tenant out of their lease and make repairs after they move out.

Ambient air testing is generally not recommended because mold is often hidden and its spores may not be at levels detectable by an ambient air sample, which is taken from the general air in a room. An air test might incorrectly suggest mold is not the cause for an odor or health complaint when it is. This is the case when mold is hidden inside a wall, ceiling, or crawlspace. If mold is present but ambient air samples do not detect it, and no action is taken to find the mold, the tenant may continue to complain and possibly become sick as nothing is done to find and correct the problem. This is not a productive path. If the mold inspector does testing, it should be with the WallChek® in places mold could be hiding.

What *Not* to Do if a Tenant Says They Smell Mold

Don't tell the tenant, "You have too good of a nose," "You're sensitive," or "No one has ever complained about mold or an odor before." Statements like that may seem helpful to assure them the problem can't be that bad, but there could be a significant and sudden leak somewhere and a significant amount of mold may be growing as a result.

How to Handle a Mold Discovery

The first thing to do is to enter the premise and smell the unit. If you don't have a good nose, you may not smell anything. That's when you should call an expert mold inspector.

What to Do if a Tenant Says They Tested for Mold

Ask for a copy of the inspection report. Check the credentials of the inspector. Verify that an accredited laboratory was used. Exclude junk science. The following are not valid ways of testing for mold. If presented with the results of one of the following types of tests, tell the tenant you will look at the results but it's not your fault money was wasted on tests which are known to give false conclusions (e.g., petri dishes, known as settling plates, and the ERMI test).

The following tests may be valid, depending on how the samples were collected and where: tape lifts, wall cavity air samples (collected using the WallChek®), and air samples. The results of tape lift samples may confirm the obvious: what you see is or is not mold. Don't get caught up with superfluous information attached to the laboratory report.

What *Not* to Do if a Tenant Says They Tested for Mold

Do not respond with, "What kind of mold is it?" or "You know, they say only certain types of mold are toxic." It doesn't matter what kind of mold is present. If mold is present it needs to be removed.

What a Tenant Should/Should Not Do and Say

What to Do if, as a Tenant, You See Mold

If you see mold, you don't need to test it. If your landlord agrees there is mold, the next step is to agree on what should be done to remove it. In the meantime, do not disturb the mold. If your landlord does not believe that what you see is mold, you will need to have it tested. Get an inspection with a report that includes recommendations for how to remove it. Make sure that any mold inspector hired does not recommend treating it. Mold should be removed, not treated.

What to Do if You Think You Smell Mold, But Don't See Mold

You need a mold inspection. It will be helpful if you can tell the mold inspector where you think it smells like mold. For mold to grow, there needs to be a source of moisture, such as a plumbing leak, a roof leak, or a leaky window. Focus the testing in that area. The inspector should use a moisture meter to check for wet spots. A WallChek® test for hidden mold should be performed on walls that are damp or suspected of hiding mold.

Common Goals

Make the Building Safe and Habitable

To achieve this goal, hire a professional mold remediator and make sure the mold is removed, not treated. Make sure the remediator follows the protocols in the *S520 Standard for Professional Mold Remediation.*

Tenants: volunteer to be the eyes and ears for your landlord to make sure the work is done correctly. Learn how mold remediation is supposed to be done, and watch the workers. The manager of the remediation company is not going to be there The supervisor will be at the office or another property preparing estimates. The workers (often day laborers) are typically left unsupervised.

Remediate Without Vacating

Tenants: you might ask the landlord to put you in a hotel while the work is being done. Part of the reason a professional mold remediation is expensive is the cost of containment. If the area with mold is properly contained, it is technically safe to occupy a building during remediation. The only thing preventing occupancy is when there is no access to a bathroom. It should be safe to continue to live in the building if an air scrubber is used to maintain a negative air pressure in the work area while remediation is being done. This assumes the air scrubber is exhausted outside, and not simply turned on inside the middle of the room and used as a big air filter.

The following will help reduce exposure to mold until remediation begins:

- A good HEPA air purifier. It must have a filter. Avoid ones that use ions or a type of technology to clean the air. They do not work and can exacerbate symptoms if anything new is introduced.
- If mold is visible, carefully cover it with plastic and tape. You may use a large plastic trash bag. Place it gently over the mold as you tape it in place.
- In rooms with visible mold, seal any heating and air conditioning vents and keep the doors to those rooms closed.
- If the mold is in a bathroom, turn the bathroom fan on (and leave it on), and then close and seal the door. The bathroom fan will suck the air out of the room, creating a suction which will help keep air in the bathroom from escaping into the occupied

space. Similarly, if mold is in the kitchen, the range hood could be turned on if the fan exhausts outside.

Minimize the Amount of Money Spent

Landlords: While it's true that you can save money by hiring a general contractor to remove the mold instead of a mold remediation company, you can't have a contractor do the work while the unit is occupied. This is because the contractor will not own an air scrubber or understand how to use it. The contractor will make a mess and spread dust around the occupied space. Next thing you know, the tenant could be asking you to pay to clean their stuff or suggest they need to throw stuff out.

One way to avoid paying a lot of money and finding out there is still mold after the remediation company says they are finished, is sharing the estimate for mold remediation with the tenant. The tenant will have to live at the property after remediation is competed. Let them be your eyes and ears. Ask if they are willing to supervise the remediation company's activities.

Pitfalls Associated
with the Goals

Making the Building Safe and Habitable

Most often, not all of the mold is removed during remediation even though it can be done. Most likely, the remediation company tried to treat the mold instead of removing it, even though they claim to follow the S520, which specifically explains why "treating" mold is not recommended. Another reason is a landlord may have chosen the cheapest company to do the work or used a handyman.

There is a small percentage of mold remediation companies that remove mold properly and completely and do not use antimicrobials or treat it. They deserve kudos. It's difficult to distinguish these companies from competitors. The quickest way to determine if a mold remediation company is competent is to ask if they'll agree to use only soap and water to clean with, and not use antimicrobials. If they say they have to use something other than soap and water, hang up.

Tenants: If you agree to not move out, you may

have to occupy the residence after remediation is completed without recourse. After your landlord spends thousands of dollars on remediation, you may have a difficult time convincing him or her that the remediation wasn't done effectively. You may have to have to hire your own inspector and pay for additional testing to be done to prove there is still mold.

Not Vacating the Property

If a landlord hires a professional to remove mold, it will be some time before the job is completed. The first step is to get estimates. Estimators will come and take measurements and go back to their offices to prepare quotes. After reviewing different offers, the landlord will approve one and choose a company. The remediation company will then put the property on their schedule. It may be weeks before they get started. Once the process begins, it may take weeks for the mold to be removed, the area re-tested, good test results achieved, and the area rebuilt.

Tenants: you will have to remain living there until the work is done. Do you have allergies? Are you immune-compromised? Do you trust the remediation company? Air scrubbers are noisy. Can you tolerate noise? The remediation company may use chemicals that create new odors, compounds that are potentially harmful or irritating — even when asked not to do so. Air purifiers will not make the situation perfect. Until remediation is complete, there may be some exposure, as mold has to travel through the air to get to the air purifier.

Tenants: If you chose to stay (not break your lease), it's recommended that you cover your stuff. Move contents into closets and seal the closets with tape. Pack things in boxes before putting them in the closets. Cover big items such as mattresses with plastic and tape, even if the bedrooms are not part of the work area. Cover cabinets with plastic and tape.

Minimizing the Costs

Getting a cheap mold inspection can add a layer of difficulty to an already unpleasant situation. If there is hidden mold, and an inspector doesn't find it, they will write in their report that there is no mold. Armed with this inaccurate information, a landlord may tell a tenant to quit complaining. A tenant then has to hire their own inspector to investigate further. If the inspector they hire finds mold, it becomes a tug of war. Each party will want to believe their report and inspector is correct. Arguments may pursue for months with no progress. The worst of these disputes reaches litigation, where incredulous amounts of money are spent on legal battles instead of efforts to find and remove the mold. In the meantime, occupants may become sick, and the dispute could move to a court where the party harmed sues for health damages. To avoid this, get the best possible, non-biased inspection and testing.

How to Handle a Mold Discovery

Tenants: you may want to hire the inspector. Most inspectors consider their reports confidential and only share them with the client who paid for them. By hiring the mold inspector, you can be certain to receive a copy of the report and the laboratory results.

Most of the time, most of the mold is not visible until after remediation begins. There can be more than meets the eye, and more work required than what was originally estimated. To make sure all the mold has been removed, an inspection and testing should occur after the remediation workers say they're finished, and before rebuilding. This is called Post-remediation Verification, and it costs money.

Tenants: before remediation begins, before you agree to continue renting instead of asking to get out of your lease, it's recommended that you require the landlord to have Post-remediation Verification testing performed. Landlords might think this type of testing is a waste of money. The logic is that if the mold was removed, there should be no point in testing afterwards. Most remediators have a hard time passing post-testing. When they fail, remediators may state it's not possible to get rid of all of the mold because mold is everywhere. Remember the phrase "mold growth" and it's definition, there should not be any mold growth after remediation.

Some property managers are quick to tell a tenant, "The owner only wants to test once: when the remediation work is finished. They don't want to have a mold inspection first." This is an error of professional judgment. Consider the scenario when there is water damage, but not visible mold. A landlord or property manager may be tempted to cut open a wall to see if there is mold. They cross their fingers and hope they don't find any.

The issue with this is cross-contamination. Unless a mold remediator sets up containment with negative air pressure, if mold is present when the wall is cut open, the workers will spread dust that contains mold spores throughout the unit, cross-contaminating the structure and its contents. The way to avoid this is to have a mold remediator set up containment with negative air pressure before cutting holes. But if there is no mold, this might be perceived as an unnecessary expense.

Landlords: in lieu of paying a remediation company to set up full containment before cutting holes to look for mold, the best solution may be to let a tenant out of their lease. Ask them to move out before cutting holes. Better yet, don't cut holes. Instead, hire a professional mold inspector to test for mold using the WallChek®.

Mold Tests
What Works and
What Doesn't

Mold Tests

Tests That Work

Tape Lifts

This test can be used to tell if what you think is mold, is actually mold. If you see mold, you can collect a sample and send it to a laboratory for confirmation. Use clear tape. It must be perfectly clear. Do not use swabs because they damage growth structures by mashing them into fragments, making it difficult for the laboratory to recognize structures as having originated from actual mold growth. The following supplies are required:

• Clear tape. The tape must be crystal clear so that light can shine through it when it is placed under a microscope. Clear packing tape works.
• Sandwich bags.
• A sharpie marker to write on the outside of the sandwich bags.

The Sampling Procedure: To ensure that you are using clean tape, begin by peeling off a piece and discarding it. To collect a sample, peel off a small piece of tape (approximately half an inch) and stick the tape to the surface with the suspect mold. Remove the tape and stick it to the inside of a sandwich bag. Do not fold the tape onto itself. Stick the tape directly to the inside of the bag. Mark on the outside of the bag the location where the sample was collected and send the samples to a lab. Request the lab perform a "direct examination" of the tape for "mold growth."

The lab will remove the tape from the bag, mount a piece on a slide, and look at it under the microscope. If they see growth, they will tell you what kind of mold is present. If there is no mold growth, they will say "No growth." It's that simple. Don't bother asking how many spores are present or how bad or big the growth is.

To learn more about tape lift samples, watch the video demonstration in my course, How to Test Visible Mold at www.academy.healthylivingspaces.com. Readers can check out this course for free — simply register for the course and use the coupon RENTMONEY at checkout.

If you send a sample to Healthy Living Spaces, I will tell you what kind of mold it is and send you a digital picture of what it looks like under the microscope. Request an analysis by contacting me through www.healthylivingspaces.com.

Tests That Work

WallChek®

If you suspect there is hidden mold in your unit, the suspect walls (or ceilings) should be tested using a method called the WallChek®. A professional mold inspector should do the testing.

Do not compare the results of a wall test to outdoor air. The purpose is to determine if there is mold in the walls, not to compare the air inside a wall cavity to outdoor air.

I had a client whose property manager refused to accept the results of wall cavity air samples which showed there was mold inside a wall. The response from the property manager was: "A sample from inside a wall is unreliable to determine if a space is habitable. We will be conducting a general air sample test which will determine if the unit is habitable and meets the requirements for a habitable space." The judge ruled the wall test was acceptable and ordered more of wall check tests to be performed.

According to the law in that state, the term "indoor mold hazard" means "any condition of mold growth on an indoor surface, building structure, or ventilation system, including mold that is within wall cavities." While a landlord might go to great lengths to encapsulate mold, legally, mold inside wall cavities is not acceptable, and this test, when performed correctly, detects it.

Tests That Don't Work

The following do not hold up to scientific scrutiny and are known to give false results in regard to the absence or presence of mold. In some cases, these tests indicate there is mold, when there is not; in others, they suggest there is not mold, when there is. Using any of these tests is counter-productive. Instead of proceeding with a discussion on what should be done to remove the mold, a landlord may dispute the results, and progress on resolving an issue may come to a halt.

Petri Dishes

These tests can be purchased at local hardware stores or online for $10 US or less. The user leaves agar plates out for a given amount of time, lets spores in the air settle on the plates, seals the plates, and sends them to a laboratory. This test can yield both false positive and false negative results.

A false positive means there is not mold growth in the building, but the results suggests there is. This occurs because the plates have agar designed to support mold growth. A few mold spores fall out of the air, land on the plate, and grow.

A false negative occurs when there is mold growth in the building, but the mold is not detected. This occurs because dead (non-viable) spores do not grow or because the agar used does not support the type of mold that is growing in the building.

There are issues regarding how the results are interpreted. There is no baseline. Some laboratories suggest there is a maximum, normal level of mold. There's no such thing. The key word is growth. There should be zero mold-growth indoors. Without an outdoor sample, you don't know what level detected is due to spores in the outdoor air at the time of testing. Leaving a dish outside to grow mold for comparison does not improve the accuracy of the test. Conditions (wind blowing, temperate, weight and bouency of spore types) affect the outcome. Lighter spore types do not settle as readily as heavier ones. To accurately collect air samples using agar plates, an Anderson-type sampling device is required with a vacuum pump calibrated to the proper flow rate, equipment that costs hundreds of dollars and requires training to operate.

The Environmental Relative Mold Index (ERMI)

The ERMI was developed by the EPA as a better

(cheaper) way for a homeowner to test for mold. A homeowner collects a sample of dust from their home and sends the it to a laboratory. The laboratory tests the dust for spores and compares the results to what is considered "normal" or, in this case, relative to the samples that were collected to establish the baseline upon which the ERMI is founded. In 2013, the Office of Investigative Government (OIG) required the EPA to release a statement that reminded people the ERMI is a research project and not intended for public use.

Understanding Air Samples

The common type of air sample collected by a mold inspector is a called a spore trap. A spore trap consists of a cassette, inside which a sticky glass slide is suspended. The cassette is attached to a vacuum pump. When the pump is turned on, air flows through the cassette and particles in the air stick to the slide. At the laboratory, an analyst removes the slide and examines the particles on the slide to determine which are mold spores and what kind and how many spores are present. Spore traps have become the normal way of collecting air samples because they are easy to collect and have a fast turnaround time. The issue is that a single spore trap (or even a few) may or may not detect mold growth in a building.

Prior to the mid-2000s, it was common to collect a second type of air sample in addition to spore traps: viable samples. Doing so tripled the cost of testing, and it took as long as ten days to receive results from the laboratory. But the confidence in making conclusions regarding the absence or presence of mold in a building was much higher. As more home inspectors became "mold inspectors," they were trained to keep things simple and their prices competitive. They were only trained to collect spore traps. Most have never heard of culturing air samples. An Anderson sampler is required to collect cultured air samples, a piece of equipment likely not found in most mold inspector's toolboxes.

Just as a doctor must choose a type of media to culture a swab taken from a nose or throat, so must a mold inspector choose which types of agar to use to collect air samples for culture. As it turns out, not all molds like the same type of food. To get accurate air sampling results, it's best to use two or three types of agar: malt or potato dextrose agar for general types of fungi; a cellulose-rich agar high in water content for molds such as *Stachybotrys;* and a third agar for actinomycetes, a group of gram-positive bacteria. Doing this right involves collecting a dozen or more air samples. The complexity and cost of this sampling strategy is one reason the EPA decided to try and create an alternative method to test for mold such as the ERMI.

The chances of determining whether there is mold in a building can be as high as 90% if you test the air using both spore traps and a variety of agar plates using an Anderson sampler. If you test using only spore traps, your likelihood of detecting mold is closer to 50%.

Before it can be concluded that there is not mold growth in a building based on air sampling, at a minimum, two of each type of sample type (spore traps and agar plates) should be collected indoors and outdoors for comparison.

Back to spore traps. If an air sample (spore trap) was collected indoors, check that an outdoor sample was collected at the same time. Without an outdoor air sample for comparison, indoor air samples cannot be evaluated. Some laboratories provide data on what types of mold are typically found outdoors. Levels fluctuate by season, time of day, relative humidity, wind, and other environmental conditions. A historical record of levels of mold outdoors cannot be used to make a conclusion as to whether mold growth is present.

If the only one air sample was collected indoors, it may not be possible to make a conclusion as to whether there is mold growth indoors. This is because there is variability in what's floating in the air past the sampling equipment any moment. I average the results of two indoor samples collected in the same location (not different rooms) and compare that to the outdoor air sample collected at the time of testing. This type of comparison provides more confidence in the results.

If a claim is made of mold growth in a building based on a single air sample, I might suggest re-testing, and taking two indoor samples in the same location. The exception is if a significant number of spores or colonies of an indicator organisms such as

Stachybotrys or *Chaetomium* were detected in the spore trap.

The complexity and cost of a trustworthy air sampling strategy is a reason the WallChek® is a preferred way of testing a building for the presence of mold growth. The pitfall is that one must be certain to test all of the walls (or floor or ceiling cavities) that have the potential hidden mold. Consider that the aforementioned air sampling strategy requires a minimum of eight to twelve (or more) samples. Imagine if instead you tested twelve walls in a building. Of course you can do both. It's just a matter of money.

Want to learn more?

The classic textbook on investigating buildings for the presence of microorganisms is *Bioaerosols: Assessment and Control* by The American Conference of Governmental Industrial Hygienists, 1999.

Points to Remember

- The only valid types of mold test are tape lifts from surfaces that appear to have mold and air samples including wall cavity air samples known as a WallChek®

- Ambient air sampling is generally not recommended as part of an investigation. Use a WallChek® to test suspect walls for hidden mold.

Air samples should only be collected for curiosity's sake or if a complete sampling regiment is used that consists of collecting both spore traps and viable (cultured) air samples.

Rights and
Responsibilities

Rent Money: Mold Handbook

Landlord Rights and Responsibilities

Even if the city or state a property is in does not have mold laws or regulations, landlords can still be held liable for mold and moisture problems under legal clauses that require rental housing to be habitable and livable. Mold needs moisture to grow. If mold has grown, there must be or have been a plumbing leak, roof leak, or other source of moisture. Since mold needs time to grow, finding mold suggests a landlord did not respond to an occurrence in a timely manner or did not make the repairs necessary to prevent it from happening again.

When to Test

If it smells like mold there's a good chance there is mold and you may not need to test. If you are confident there is not mold, it may be prudent to have some air testing done for due diligence. Collect a few indoor air samples to document the conditions and show that you made an effort to investigate and found nothing.

If you pay for a mold test and the consultant collecting the samples gives you a report that states something such as: "Findings reflect acceptable levels and that no further action is recommended," be prepared to have it challenged. There is no such thing as an acceptable level of mold. If you get a report that says: "All of the numbers reported were acceptable," you are getting bad advice.

The indoor samples should be compared to the outdoor samples. If they're similar, then the report should say they are similar. There's no need to use the word "acceptable" or "normal," and doing so implies a lack of understanding of how the results should be interpreted. If the inspector thinks there is not mold growth indoors based on the laboratory results, the correct language to use is something such as: "Results do not indicate amplification (differences) of fungal spores in the indoor air relative to the outdoor reference sample collected at the time of testing." This does not mean, "There is no mold growth in the building."

What to Consider if There is Mold

Consider if you want the headache. It may be easier to let a tenant out of a lease. If they get sick because you didn't take action, or didn't take action fast enough, your liability can increase. Instead of finding yourself in court simply disputing what is owed on the lease, it may escalate to a court where tenants can sue for damages to health. Some attorneys say it's difficult to prove exposure to mold. The same attorneys also win big money for clients who say they got sick. Either way, it's a long and expensive road in attorney fees for both parties. If the tenant says they want their deposit back and out of their lease, and you suspect they are being honest about the presence of mold, it may be in your best interest to let them go. These cases usually settle, which means the rent is the least you could lose.

Going to Court

Before making the decision to go to court, I recommend you make friends with the tenant, offer to give them their deposit back, and part ways amicably instead. Consider having them sign something that says you are not liable for any health effects they might later claim.

In small claims court, it is my experience that a judge will not want to hear about health effects, rather they will want to hear what part of the contract, lease agreement, or tenant/land-lord law has been violated. If you are keeping the deposit, make sure you give the tenant line items for expenses within the time required by law. I saw a case where the mold was caused by the tenants and the landlord simply kept all of the deposit because it was going to cost more to remove the mold than the amount of the deposit. The judge found for the tenant because the landlord did not provide a written list of the cost of the damages within the required time frame.

If your tenant says their health has been damaged, the case will likely go to a higher court for personal injury litigation. There will be a discovery process, depositions will be taken, and a settlement will be reached. Be prepared to come to a settlement. Rarely do cases go to trial. Lawyers often claim there is no proof mold causes illness. I've had the same attorneys tell me they win big for those that claim they got sick from mold exposure. As an expert witness, I have become disenchanted with the legal process.

Tenant Rights and Responsibilities

Obey the Lease

If there is mold, a landlord might decide to terminate your lease (and not remove the mold) because you violated it for other reasons. A common one is having a pet when pets are not allowed, or having more pets than what your lease allows. In that case, even though you have a right to a safe and habitable living space, the property manager may sue you for violating the lease and be able to keep your deposit, even though there is mold.

Request the Standard of Care

The following was required by an apartment manager, prepared by the Apartment Association of the state in which the unit is located. At first glance, it seems like they are trying to educate renters about how mold grows, how to prevent it, and what to do if mold is found, which is a good thing. The document, however,

Mold Information and Prevention Addendum

Please note: It is our goal to maintain a quality living environment for our residents. To help achieve this goal, it is important to work together to minimize any mold growth in your dwelling. That is why this addendum contains important information for you, and responsibilities for both you and us.

1. **ADDENDUM.** This is an addendum to the Lease or Rental Agreement executed by you, the resident(s), on the dwelling you have agreed to rent. That dwelling is:

   Apt# ▮▮▮▮

   at ▮▮▮▮ Apartments

   (name of apartments)

   or other dwelling located at ▮▮▮▮

   (street address)

   City/State where dwelling is located ▮▮▮▮

2. **ABOUT MOLD:** Mold is found virtually everywhere in our environment - both indoors and outdoors and in both new and old structures. Molds are naturally occurring microscopic organisms which reproduce by spores and have existed practically from the beginning of time. All of us have lived with mold spores all our lives. Without mold we would all be struggling with large amounts of dead organic matter.

   Mold breaks down organic matter in the environment and uses the end product for its food. Mold spores (like plant pollen) spread through the air and are commonly transported by shoes, clothing, and other materials. When excess moisture is present inside a dwelling, mold can grow. There is conflicting scientific evidence as to what constitutes a sufficient accumulation of mold which could lead to adverse health effects. Nonetheless, appropriate precautions need to be taken.

3. **PREVENTING MOLD BEGINS WITH YOU.** In order to minimize the potential for mold growth in your dwelling, you must do the following:
   - Keep your dwelling clean - - particularly the kitchen, the bathroom(s), carpets, and floors. Regular vacuuming, mopping and using a household cleaner to clean hard surfaces is important to remove the household dirt and debris that harbor mold or food for mold. Immediately throw away moldy food.
   - Remove visible moisture accumulation on windows, walls, ceilings, floors and other surfaces as soon as reasonably possible. Look for leaks in washing machine hoses and discharge lines - - especially if the leak is large enough for water to infiltrate nearby walls. Turn on any exhaust fans in bathroom and kitchen before you start showering or cooking with open pots. When showering, be sure to keep the shower curtain inside the tub or fully close the shower doors. Also, the area we recommend that after taking a shower or bath, you: (1) wipe moisture off all shower walls, shower doors, the bathtub and the bathroom floor; (2) leave the bathroom door open until all moisture on the mirrors and bathroom walls and tile surfaces has dissipated; and (3) hang up your towels and bath mats so they will completely dry out.
   - Promptly notify us in writing about any air conditioning or heating system problems you discover. Follow our rules, if any, regarding replacement of air filters. Also, it is recommended that you periodically open windows and doors on days when the outdoor weather is dry (i.e. humidity is below 50 percent) to help humid areas of your dwelling dry out.
   - Promptly notify us in writing about any signs of water leaks, water infiltration or mold. We will respond in accordance with state law and the Rental Agreement to repair or remedy the situation, as necessary.

4. **IN ORDER TO AVOID MOLD GROWTH,** it is important to prevent excessive moisture buildup in your dwelling. Failure to promptly pay attention to leaks and moisture that might accumulate on dwelling surfaces or that might get inside walls or ceilings can encourage mold growth. Prolonged moisture can result from a wide variety of sources, such as:
   - rainwater leaking from roofs, windows, doors and outside walls, as well as flood waters rising above floor level;
   - overflows from showers, bathtubs, toilets, lavatories, sinks, washing machines, humidifiers, dehumidifiers, refrigerator or A/C drip pans or clogged up A/C condensation lines;
   - leaks from plumbing lines or fixtures, and leaks into walls from bad or missing grouting/caulking around showers, tubs, or sinks;
   - washing machines hose leaks, plant watering overflows, pet urine, cooking spills, beverage spills and steam from excessive open-pot cooking;
   - leaks from clothes dryer discharge vents (which can put lots of moisture into the air); and
   - insufficient drying of carpets, carpet pads, shower walls and bathroom floors.

5. **IF SMALL AREAS OF MOLD HAVE ALREADY OCCURRED** ON NON-POROUS SURFACES (such as ceramic tile, Formica®, vinyl flooring, metal, wood or plastic), the federal Environmental Protection Agency (EPA) recommends that you first clean the areas with soap (or detergent) and water, let the surface dry, and then within 24 hours apply a premixed, spray-on-type household biocide, such as Lysol Disinfectant®, Pine-Sol Disinfectant® (original pine-scented), Tilex Mildew Remover® or Clorox Cleanup® (Note: Only a few of the common household cleaners will actually kill mold). Tilex® and Clorox® contain bleach which can discolor or stain. Be sure to follow the instructions on the container. Applying biocides without first cleaning away the dirt and oils from the surface is like painting over old paint without first cleaning and preparing the surface.

   Always clean and apply a biocide to an area 5 or 6 times larger than any visible mold because mold may be adjacent in quantities not yet visible to the naked eye. A vacuum cleaner with a high-efficiency particulate air (HEPA) filter can be used to help remove non-visible mold products from porous items, such as fibers in sofas, chairs, drapes and carpets - - provided the fibers are completely dry. Machine washing or dry cleaning will remove mold from clothes.

6. **DO NOT CLEAN OR APPLY BIOCIDES TO:** (1) visible mold on porous surfaces, such as sheetrock walls or ceilings, or (2) large areas of visible mold on non-porous surfaces. Instead, notify us in writing, and we will take appropriate action in compliance with state law, subject to special exceptions for natural disasters.

7. **COMPLIANCE.** Complying with this addendum will help prevent mold growth in your dwelling, and both you and we will be able to respond correctly if problems develop that could lead to mold growth. If you have questions regarding this addendum, please contact us at the management office or at the phone number shown in your Rental Agreement.

   If you fail to comply with this Addendum, you can be held responsible for property damage to the dwelling and any health problems that may result. We can't fix problems in your dwelling unless we know about them.

   This is a binding legal document. Your signature means that you have read, understood and agreed to the provisions set out above. You are entitled to receive a copy of this Addendum after it is fully signed. Keep in a safe place.

   OWNER/AGENT ▮▮▮▮   RESIDENT (s) (All residents must sign here) ▮▮▮▮

   DATE: ▮▮▮▮   DATE: ▮▮▮▮

states that should mold be discovered, the renter agrees to actions contrary to what is found in the standard of care for professional mold remediation. All of the information in Section 5 is contrary to the normally accepted standard of care. The EPA does not recommend using biocides. In fact, it's proper to say "Don't clean or apply biocides." There are no household cleaners that kill mold. A vacuum cleaner cannot be used to remove mold *growth*. Washing clothes will not remove mold *growth*.

If I were a renter presented with this, I would pencil in the following: "All Owner/Agent activities will comply with what is written in the S520 Professional Standard for Mold Remediation."

Ironically, the client who showed me this document had mold in their apartment. The maintenance staff treated the mold with a biocide instead of removing it and claimed they were in compliance with state laws.

Sample Letter

If you have had a mold inspection, verified mold is present and mold remediation is required, but believe your landlord is not going to remediate the mold properly, you might want to consider moving. The following is an example of a letter you might write:

Dear _____,

Rather than continue this process, I've decided to take you up on your offer to let me out of the lease. Based on what I'm hearing from you vs. my inspector, I don't see us getting on the same page. Please prepare a lease termination agreement and a check refunding my pro-rated rent for this month and security deposit. Let me know when to pass by your office to finish doing business and return the keys.

Going to Court

It's unfortunate when a dispute cannot be resolved, and parties turn to litigation. Unless you are suing for health damages, you'll likely be going to small claims court to break your lease and get your deposit back. People can represent themselves, it's just a matter of being proficient at understanding the housing laws, not mold laws. Most states do not have mold laws, and in those that do, the laws may not be applicable to rental properties.

It's my experience the judge will not want to hear as much about health effects and what kind of mold is present, as what part of the contract, lease agreement, or tenant/land-lord law has been violated. A judge will be looking for something to hang their hat on in regard to something clearly spelled out in the law. An example might be if the landlord did not return your deposit in a timely manner.

If you feel your health has been damaged, you may want to hire an attorney and file a lawsuit in a higher court. Lawsuits can drag on for years. It will help your case to have a mold inspection by someone with proper certification. Your mold inspector is not a doctor. Legally, one can only be an expert in one area at any given time in the courtroom. Have a doctor diagnose your illness. When a doctor can testify that your illness is due to the mold that the mold inspector found, that's a solid case.

A mold attorney, one who specializes in mold, is not required. They may have formed their own, non-expert opinions, some of which will be based on misinformation. You simply need a good attorney. Depending on the case, it might be one who specializes in personal injury law, tenant/landlord law, or contracts.

How to Find a Mold-free Rental

Step 1

Don't base your search on the part of town an apartment or house is located. Any building of any age is capable of having mold growth. It's common to have windows leak in newer buildings because the window openings are not flashed correctly. Old craftsman homes can be a good bet. If an older house looks well-maintained, it might be as good of a bet as a newer home. Older homes are often built with care and made with plaster and lath instead of drywall. The paper-backing on drywall (wallboard) used to build interior walls in modern homes (starting in the 1950s) loves to grow mold when it gets wet. Older houses with cement plaster may not have drywall.

As discussed in, *What Your Builder Should Know - Best Practices for Building a Healthy Home,* avoid housing with crawlspaces and basements. Find one built on a concrete slab (referred to as slab-on-grade). Ask a potential landlord if there has ever been a leak, flood, or visible mold in the house, and if so, how repairs and remediation were performed.

Step 2

Ask to see the property. If the unit has been closed up (the windows are closed) and it smells like mold, there is no point in considering it. If the windows and doors are suspiciously wide open, it's possible the landlord is trying to make it smell cleaner than it is. If there is an odor from fragrance, air-fresheners, candles, or incense, reschedule the showing and request the windows be closed the night before and that there not be anything fragrant during the showing.

Step 3

Do your own mold inspection. Half the time, mold that is growing is readily visible. Mold needs water to grow. Check places with the potential for plumbing leaks and where water may have leaked in from the outside. Search the following places for mold or water damage:
- Under kitchen sinks at the back wall inside the cabinet.
- Walls next to and behind a dishwasher.
- Walls next to and behind a refrigerator/freezer with an ice maker.

- In bedroom closets that have exterior walls, near floor level on the exterior walls.
- In bedroom closets opposite showers and bathtubs.
- At the back wall under (inside) bathroom sink vanities.
- On the walls behind and next to toilets.
- Inside the hot water heater closet at the walls next to and behind the water heater. Look at the floor for evidence of water damage, leaks, and repairs.
- If there is a forced air heating system or air conditioning, find the system and inspect the air filters. While doing so, look inside for evidence of water damage and mold. In units where the system sits on a platform and the return air vent is on the front of the platform, remove the vent cover and look in the space under the platform.
- On ceilings — look for stains from roof leaks or from a shower or toilet on the upper floor. Look for water marks, discolorations, evidence of patching, painting, and cracks.
- On windowsills and on walls under windows, look for evidence of the windows leaking or being left open during rain.
- If there is carpet, pull up the edge of the carpet under windows and look at the carpet tacks. If the carpet tacks are rust colored, stained, or have mold, the windows may have leaked or be leaking.
- If there is a crawlspace, wear a respirator, put on disposable coveralls, and look for wet soil, plumb-

ing leaks, and mold.
- Peek your head inside attics.

Make a habit of looking in every closet and access panel that can be opened. Mold is often found in places people infrequently look.

If it's raining, use a moisture meter to check walls under the corners of windows. A moisture meter can be purchased at a local hardware store for $50. Press the pins into the wall under the corners of the windows. Readings 17% or higher suggest the wall is damp; readings 20% or greater indicate the wall is wet.

If you find something suspicious, ask the landlord about it. Take pictures. You can send them to me and we can do a phone consultation.

Step 4

Have a professional mold inspection, which may include testing the air and testing walls that are suspicious for hidden mold. Most landlords will allow a potential renter to pay to have a mold inspection. Some will tell you they don't want to know what the inspector finds or what the laboratory results are. They may allow you to test and inspect under the condition you get back to them with a simple "yes" or "no" in regard to if you want to rent the property. It may take a week or longer for you to schedule an inspection and to get results from the laboratory. Unless a landlord is highly interested in having you as a tenant, he or she may not hold the property for you as you wait for the test results and make a decision.

Step 5

The best way to tell if a property is going to affect your health is to occupy it. Ask if you can spend the night. Keep the windows closed. Trust your instincts and your body. If you feel good spending the night, confirm your gut feeling that there is not mold with the results of the professional mold inspection and testing results.

Mold Remediation Company Responsibilities

The Standard of Care

The standard of care for mold remediation can be found in the *IICRC S520 Standard for Professional Mold Remediation.* It contains definitions regarding what should and should not be done. Where the term "shall" is used, it means there is a law behind what's written. When the term "should" is used, it means the practice or procedure is a component of the accepted standard of care that must be followed, whether or not it's mandated by law. When the term "recommended" is used, it means the practice or procedure is advised or suggested, but is not a component of the accepted standard of care.

Most remediation companies say they follow the S520. Many remediation companies are certified by the IICRC to perform mold remediation and display IICRC logos on their websites, letterheads, and vehicles. According to IICRC policy, said certification holders and use of logos requires an awareness and knowledge about IICRC's published standards and guidelines.

In cases where mold remediation is not preformed properly, an attorney might ask an expert, "Did the Defendant [the mold remediation company] breach the standard of care? If so, how?" To answer that question, reference the S520. The following are a few examples of how a mold remediation company might breach the standard of care.

Not Removing the Mold

According to the S520, source removal *should* be the primary method of remediation. That means moldy drywall must be removed and the exposed wood framing cleaned by wire brushing, sanding, or other mechanical means. If the mold is painted over, treated, killed, or otherwise covered up, the standard of care has been breached. If ozone or products are used in an attempt to kill mold, the standard of care has been breached.

Using Biocides

According to the S520, the indiscriminate use of antimicrobials is *not recommended.* There are some cases when antimicrobials are appropriate, such as a sewage backup. A sanitizer may be used at the start of remediation in this case to make the area safer for workers by reducing their potential exposure to infectious diseases. However, it is not appropriate (and violates the standard of care) to use them routinely. There should be a documented specific reason for using biocides and the product used must be one that is applicable to the organism that is a threat — an organism that cannot be safely remediated without using the product. When used, the product should be applied at the start of remediation, not after workers have started to remove affected materials.

Regardless of whether a remediator chooses to follow the recommendation to not use antimicrobials, according to the standard of care, the remediator *shall* obtain a written informed consent with the customer's signature before applying an antimicrobial.

I was once asked in a deposition, "But don't most mold remediators use antimicrobials?"

I answered, "Yes."

The attorney suggested that meant it must be OK. I replied that it was similar to speeding — just because a lot of people drive over the posted speed limit does not make it legal.

When I ask remediators why they use antimicrobials, they often reply, "We have to."

When I ask them why, they usually say they are following the S520 standard. The truth is either they have not read the S520, or they have a poor memory. When I offer them the opportunity to demonstrate that they are correct by asking what page in the standard states they should use antimicrobials, they are unable to answer.

Mold Remediation

Mold Remediation

What Does Not Remove Mold

Let's say you want to do the right thing and get rid of the mold. It's not as simple as just writing a check to a remediation company and having it go away. You have to watch the remediation company and read the estimate. If you don't, chances are there will be still be mold even after the mold remediation company tells you they are finished. This is because the workers think they can kill it instead of remove it, even though the intention with the service is to remove it. The following so-called "solutions" do not remove mold and are therefore a waste of effort, time, and money.

Antimicrobials, Disinfectants, Sanitizers, Bleach

Bleach is effective at killing bacteria when dissolved in water; however, ions rappel from hard surfaces. If there is any doubt as to how ineffective bleach is, try cleaning a dirty floor with bleach.

What Does Not Remove Mold

Mold Bomb Foggers

These do not kill or remove mold. After detecting mold in an inspection I did for a tenant, the landlord allowed the tenant to move out. A few weeks later, I received a letter from the landlord: "Before we rent the unit to another tenant, I was wondering: Since the crawl space and wall cavity areas you detected mold in are inaccessible, what do you think of bombing it with this product. Would it help?" I told the landlord fragrance and chemicals are tip-offs that an attempt was made to treat or cover up mold, so it's a bad idea. There's no such thing as an inaccessible space. It just might cost more in some cases to cut into a floor or wall to make sure you removed the mold.

Special Paint

If a landlord tells a tenant to clean and paint over mold, they may get a notice like this from the tenant: "I'm writing to let you know that we are struggling with a severe mold problem. This is the fourth time the mold has come back. Each time the mold comes back faster. The last two times we removed it with bleach and water and painted with a product called Kilz, a mold-resistant paint. It's been two weeks and you can see that it's come back. We tried scraping the mold off and coating it, but it has returned with a vengeance."

Not Good Enough

For mold to be visible, a surface must contain a minimum of one million spores per square inch. Imagine there is a spot of mold visible. Imagine spraying it with an antimicrobial that claims to kill 99.9%. Assuming one million spores are present, the treatment will leave 1,000 viable mold spores. Depending on the type of antimicrobial or disinfectant used, the competing organisms may be killed, allowing the 1,000 remaining spores to thrive — per square inch.

What Works

As explained in more detail in my book *Mold Money: How to Save Thousands of Dollars on Mold Remediation and Make Sure the Mold is Gone*, drywall that has mold on it needs to be removed. Use a wire bush and soap and water to clean the exposed wood framing after the drywall is removed. If there are cabinets in the way, they need to come out to remove drywall behind them. The following is a summary:

1. Set up "containment"

Plastic should be hung, floor to ceiling, to isolate the work area from the rest of the living space. An air scrubber should be placed in the middle of the work area. The exhaust duct from the scrubber must go to the outside, though a door or window. I tape a big piece of cardboard over a window opening and cut a hole in it to insert the exhaust duct. The idea is to make the room/work area airtight and create suction, like a big vacuum cleaner. Set up properly, the air scrubber (also known as a negative air machine) will suck the dust (and mold) in the air out of the room and exhaust it outside, preventing dust from escaping and contaminating the rest of the unit. The scrubber has a HEPA filter to capture the dust (and mold) so the neighbors can't complain.

I received the following letter from a property manager who hired a professional remediation company to remove the mold in a unit using full containment with negative air pressure: "The owner of this property has asked if you could write a letter regarding the mold. She wants to be able to tell the tenant that they can live there without breaking the lease."

Since I knew the remediation company, had experience checking their work, and was certain that an air scrubber was going to be used and set up properly, I wrote back: "In reference to the mold remediation at_____, the unit is habitable during remediation."

2. Pull out what's in the way

Typically, most mold is hidden and remains invisible until the drywall is cut out. If the leak that caused the mold is in a kitchen or bathroom for example, cabinets may need to be pulled out to remove the mold in the walls behind them. The cabinets may have mold on the bottom or backs in places not visible for inspection until they are removed.

Cabinets should be wrapped in plastic before being removed from the work area. Take them outside where you can determine if they can be salvaged or should be discarded. If it's just a kickplate or the back side of a cabinet that's moldy, the pieces can be replaced during the rebuild. When in doubt, throw it out. Mold is microscopic. Don't assume there is not mold unless you collect surface samples, something a mold inspector can do.

3. Cut it out

Cut out drywall that is moldy on walls and ceilings. Cut drywall out in a two-feet perimeter around where it looks moldy or wet or stained on the back side. Cut out any rot. This may mean cutting out sections of flooring, sill plates (the bottom piece of wood a wall is framed with), plywood on exterior walls, and the bottom of roof decking that is visible once drywall on a ceiling is cut out. Most general contractors will tell you it's easier to cut than clean. That's because they are better at cutting than cleaning. When given a choice, allow them to cut stuff out versus expecting them to adequately clean the mold off a surface.

4. Sand and wire brush

The remaining wood that is exposed (framing, exterior sheathing, the bottom of roof decking, sill plates, and so forth) and hard surfaces such as block and concrete, should be wire brushed. A wire brush works better than a sander. Use a sander for large, flat areas. For small areas and corners of framing, use a wire brush. Use a wire brush on block walls and on concrete floors. All this is done with the air scrubber running and negative air pressure so that the dust gets sucked out of the air as soon as it's produced.

5. Vacuum

Clean the entire work area; HEPA vacuum everything. Vacuum the insides of wall and ceiling cavities, framing, along the bottom of sill plates, walls, the floor, and so forth. This is a weak point for many.

6. Blow

A vacuum cleaner by itself is not be effective at removing dust and mold particles in hard-to-reach places. Some contractors use a compressed air hose to blow dust out of nooks and crannies. Using a compressed air hose is working harder, not smarter. Use a leaf blower. It's a shotgun approach — blow everything. Aim the blower at walls, floors, and exposed wood framing where drywall has been removed. The blowing should be done with the air scrubber exhausting outside, so that a negative air pressure (suction) is maintained. The remediator should walk though, blowing with the leaf blower, then go outside and wait fifteen minutes for the dust to settle. After fifteen minutes, they should go back inside, vacuum the big stuff off the floor, and then repeat the blowing and vacuuming cycle until no big stuff blows out.

7. Wipe

After vacuuming, damp wipe everything. Use plain soap and water. The objective is to clean up the dust. There should not be any mold remaining except for what's in the dust. Bleach does a poor job of cleaning because it does not have a surfactant. Dish soap works great. Lots of rags are required. A clean rag should be dipped in soapy water and rung out to remove most of the water. Dirty rags should not go back into the sudsy water. Damp wipe all the surfaces, including exposed wood framing, sill plates, and so forth. It also includes the ceiling, walls, and floor. When completed, the room should look and smell clean. If it does not, you likely missed something.

8. Test

Have a mold inspection before you rebuild. If the walls are rebuilt before the mold test, the test will not be accurate. I once had to tell a client to tear a wall down a second time after the handyman had remediated and rebuilt it twice before I could inspect it because the lab results indicated there was still mold. The handyman's idea of removing the mold and cleaning was not up to par. It would have been easier and cheaper for everyone if the mold inspection had been done before he started rebuilding it the first time.

Examples

Mold on the Ceiling in a Shower

In the case of mold growing on the ceiling in a shower from condensation, the mold is only growing on the surface — there's no mold hiding inside the ceiling. Most of the mold may stay wet and sticky, and may not become airborne. Since the mold is just growing on the surface, the quick solution is to wipe it off. Dish soap works best. Don't bother using bleach.

To prevent this from happening, install a bathroom fan. Wire the fan to the light switch on the bathroom wall so that it turns on any time someone is in the bathroom. This is what hotels do — they run the fans all the time or connect them to a motion detector.

Typically condensation occurs in the wintertime. For humid air to condense requires humidity and cold surfaces. The colder a surface is, the more condensation there will be. Sometimes a lack of insulation in a wall or ceiling can be a factor. When rebuilding or remodeling, installing a sheet of rigid insulation on the backside of the ceiling will help keep surfaces warmer.

If there continues to be condensation, the mold will grow back even faster after the cleaning. This is because the organism has roots growing into the substrate — the drywall or plaster. The drywall will need to be cut out to get the roots. Repaint the ceiling with a product used by mold remediation companies to encapsulate mold, such as Safe Encasement Systems, whose main ingredient is boric acid.

Normal kitchen and bathroom paints, including those many believe will kill mold, have added antimicrobials. That's what makes them special compared to normal paint. But the antimicrobial chemicals don't last long because they off-gas. It's best to use a product made to encapsulate mold instead of killing it.

Concrobium and similar products can useful for the scenario where mold is only growing on the surface and the surface is dry so that additional mold can not grow. Products like this encapsulate mold with a clear, invisible coating that locks the spores and other growth particles down. If you try to scrape the mold off after applying the product, you won't be able to. So make sure the surface is as clean and dry as possible before applying it. These types of products are also sold with foggers to treat areas that are inaccessible but that doesn't work because the fog is not under enough pressure to coat surfaces in hidden and inaccessible places.

Be sure that the mold and staining on the ceiling are due only to condensation, and there's no plumbing leak in the roof or ceiling. If there's a leak from above, you must cut the ceiling out to dry and remove the mold on the other side. Encapsulating the visible surface is just prolonging the inevitable by leaving serious mold growth where it's not visible.

Shower tiles present a similar scenario — the mold that is growing may only be cosmetic. If, however, water penetrates cracks or missing grout and gets into the walls, a lot of hidden and potentially bad types of mold can grow. In the worst-case scenario, a complete gut of the shower may be required. To prevent this, inspect and repair cracks in tile grout and missing sealant as soon as possible.

Mold Behind a Kitchen Sink Cabinet

If mold is found growing on the wall behind a sink cabinet, the only way to remove the mold is to remove the cabinet so you can remove any affected drywall behind it as well. Most of the mold will be at the bottom (i.e., the place that got the wettest and stayed wet the longest) where it's not visible for inspection. Encapsulants are not going to be useful in this case. To prevent this, make sure the backsplash is caulked. If you're remodeling, install a one-piece-type sink that includes a backsplash.

If the cabinets themselves are not moldy or only partially contaminated, you may consider reusing them. You will have to remove them to cut the drywall out behind them. You may either replace the affected parts of the cabinets or try to remove the mold on them by sanding. If you choose to sand them, take them outside and wear a respirator. I would not suggest painting the cabinets just to be sure that you removed all the mold. If you can't get to the surfaces to clean them (i.e., nooks and crannies between pieces of wood) paint won't get in there either. A practical example of reusing cabinets is when only the bottom surface (the kickplates) are moldy and you've replaced these parts after you removed the cabinets and removed the moldy drywall behind them.

Carpet

When carpet gets wet, it needs to be dried within two days to prevent mold growth. Dry means a reading of 15% or less with a moisture meter. If a carpet has mold growth, it should be replaced. Cleaning is not effective. When carpet is replaced, the tacks and padding should also be replaced. If there is a wood subfloor under the carpet, inspect the wood. If the wood is discolored or moldy, after the wood is dry, sand and wire brush it to make sure it's clean before installing new padding and carpet.

Want to learn more?

Buy a copy of *Mold Money: How to Save Thousands of Dollars on Mold Remediation and Make Sure the Mold is Gone*. It contains examples of logbooks, worksheets, and checklists, as well as information on how to read estimates, what to look for when supervising remediation workers, and how to do remediation yourself.

Points to Remember

- Mold growth needs to be removed, not treated. Remove mold according to what is suggested in the *ANSI/IICRC S520 Standard for Professional Mold Remediation.*

The Mold Inspection Process

The Mold Inspection Process

How to Find a
Good Mold Inspector

There are two types of inspectors: those you call if you don't want to find mold, and those you call if you want an unbiased assessment. A landlord may tell an inspector, "Please don't find mold." A tenant might tell an inspector, "Can you tell me where the mold is," i.e., "I am sure you are going to find mold, otherwise you're not doing your job."

The easiest way to find a mold inspector with credible credentials is to look on the American Council for Accredited Certification (ACAC) website. The ACAC is the only third-party, accredited certification body. Go to ACAC.org, enter your zip code, and look for a Certified Microbial Consultant (CMC). Next, call three candidates and ask about their experience. Ask to see their CV (curriculum vitae is a legal term for a resume). Then select the one with whom you feel most comfortable.

Beware of mold inspectors who have a certificate from taking an online course. According to the definition of certification, it requires some form of external review, i.e., an independent process by a third party, not just taking a class. If a certification is not accredited, it's a considered a certificate for completion of a course, not certification.

Do not hire a Certified Industrial Hygienist (CIH) unless they are also a Certified Microbial Consultant (CMC). A CIH's formal training is limited to industrial and occupational settings. Most CIHs have not been trained to do mold inspections. To weed out the CIHs with relevant experience, request a CV and a list of textbooks on their bookshelf. The ACAC lists text books on their website next to the certification requirements. These are considered industry standards. A competent professional should own copies of the following:

- *Bioaerosols: Assessment and Control.* Janet Macher, Ed., American Conference of Governmental Industrial Hygienists, (1999).
- *Field Guide for the Determination of Biological Contaminants in Environmental Samples.* American Industrial Hygiene Association, (1996).
- *ANSI/IICRC S520-2015 Standard for Professional Mold Remediation.* Institute of Inspection, Cleaning and Restoration Certification (IICRC).

What a Mold Inspector Should Do

1. Perform a visual inspection

The inspector should first look for visible mold and signs of water damage. They should use a moisture meter. They should inspect the heating, ventilation, and air conditioning (HVAC) system. Where mold, moisture, or water damage are evident but mold is not, the inspector should note the need for further investigation and testing.

They should not cut holes to look for mold or attempt to snake a camera or boroscope through the holes to look for mold. Mold is microscopic. Cameras and boroscopes are not microscopes. Often these places are too dark to discern if what looks like mold is mold, or if what looks clean is clean. I found using a boroscope so unreliable, that I sold mine. I only kept it as long as I did because potential clients often asked if I had one.

2. Test as needed

If mold is visible, the inspector may collect a surface sample (tape lift). It's not necessary to know what kind of mold is present to begin remediation. This type of testing is only to know for certain that what looks like mold is actually mold.

If mold is not visible, after making a list of the areas that have the potential for mold to be hiding, the inspector may ask you to decide which ones you would like to have tested. There will be a laboratory fee associated with each wall tested. After considering the budget and likely places mold might be hiding, the inspector should perform the testing and send the samples to a laboratory

The inspector should not use only an infrared camera (IR) to look for moisture and mold. IR cameras are heat cameras, not mold or moisture meters. The principle behind this is that wet spots are usually cooler, therefore, if we look for cool spots, we'll find mold. Water holds heat. Hot spots can be wet too. Cold and hot spots can be due to lack of insulation, direct sunlight, air duct air currents, and so forth. Too often I see mold inspection reports where the inspector incorrectly stated a surface was wet or moldy because it looked suspicious on the camera. Inspectors should always use a moisture meter to be sure.

Provide a written report

Some mold inspectors just place a cover letter on the laboratory report and hand it to their client. I consider that a poor report. Some inspectors provide generic, cookie-cutter recommendations on how to remove mold. I consider that poor service.

A good inspection report should be specific about where mold has been found (and not found) and what should be done to remove any mold that has been found. It should provide specific instructions on what to do for each place mold is found. It should include information how to interpret the enclosed laboratory results. It should document places that have the potential for mold to be present in areas that were not tested. It should note the scope of work for the remediation company. It should note areas with water damage (staining or suspect mold) in addition to those with obvious visible mold. And it should note the presence of any musty odors.

Standard Guide for Assessment of Fungal Growth in Building (D7338-10). ASTM International, 2010.

Measuring the Level of Moisture in the Air

I often get calls from those worried there is a source of moisture in their unit because the relative humidity is high. They have some predetermined level of humidity, above which they think mold can be grow. Some think it is between 40-60%. It's not that simple.

Relative humidity (RH) means relative to the temperature. RH is how much moisture air can hold at a given temperature. To know how much moisture is in the air, you must also measure the temperature. Using the RH and the temperature, you can then calculate the grains per pound of moisture (GPP) in the air. But even calculating that still won't tell you if the moisture level is too high — you must also measure the temperature and relative humidity of the outside air.

Use two instruments. Place one outside and leave it there. Note: it may take an hour or longer for readings to stabilize and be accurate. If you take a reading indoors and then take the instruments outdoors to measure, you will get inaccurate results.

It used to be that we had to use a slide ruler to calculate GPP. Now there are apps. A free one is

The Mold Inspection Process

PsychCheck, a psychrometric calculator provided by Drieaz. Enter the air temperature (Ta) and relative humidity (RH), press OK, and check the output for the grains of moisture per pound of dry air, or GPP. Repeat the process, entering the temperature and relative humidity readings for the outdoor air, and then compare the two.

The GPP should be the same indoors and outdoors. If an air conditioning unit is operating, the indoor GPP might be slightly lower than outside, as air conditioners dehumidify. If you find the GPP is higher indoors compared to outside, you have a source of moisture indoors. Determine what it is and take steps to lower the amount of moisture in the air indoors.

....

Moisture Control Handbook. Principles and Practices for Residential and Small Commercial Buildings. Joseph Lstiburek and John Carmody. John Wiley & Sons, Inc., 1994.

What a Mold Inspector Should Not Do

Don't allow an inspector to cut holes to look for mold. Cutting holes can lead to the wrong conclusions, makes a mess, and, when mold is present, exposes the occupants and their belongings to mold. Mold is microscopic and not visible without a microscope. If you cut a hole and don't see mold, that does not mean mold isn't there. A mold inspector should use the WallChek® method to test for hidden mold, not cut holes.

Points to Remember
- To find a mold inspector, look on the website for the American Council for Accredited Certification (ACAC.org), enter your zip code, and look for a Certified Microbial Consultant (CMC).

- Don't cut holes to look for hidden mold. Use the WallChek®.

Commercial Buildings

Commercial Buildings

Introduction

The types of mold that grow in commercial buildings are no different than those grow in residences. The same methods for testing and the same standards and guidelines for removing mold apply.

If you are a landlord, keep the process open. Share information with the tenants. When the inspector arrives, encourage tenants to ask questions. By sharing what you know and what is being done, you demonstrate you are trying to do the right thing and not hide something. Build trust from the start. If you start with trust, all you have to do is keep it. If you have the mold inspection done under clandestine conditions (when no one is in the office), you will start with suspicion and will have to build trust.

When there is open communication and honest disclosure, people tend to lose interest. Whereas there might be some initial worry about mold, as information is shared about what is found and not found, about what will be done to fix the problems identified and how any mold found will be removed, people start to trust management and lose interest. When they feel kept in the dark, rumors spread and panic ensues. Lacking factual information, people are left to their creative imaginations, and gossip determines what's going on. They fear the worst.

If you keep an open line of communication going, office staff should say something like the following to those that ask if they are worried that there is mold in the building: "Yes, we have mold in one part of the building. Management is taking the best steps to remove it. It's safe to work in my office while the work is being done. I'm not worried."

Testing for Mold

Don't cut holes to look for mold. Cutting holes to look for mold creates a big mess while also potentially exposing staff to dust and mold. Since mold is not visible without a microscope, mold inspectors who cut holes often do not see it and they may say there isn't mold when there is. The WallChek® was created as a better way to test commercial buildings. It allows an inspector to determine where mold is and where it stops without cutting holes. It enables an inspector to write a remediation plan that designates which cubicles and offices need to be vacated and which do not.

HVAC Systems

Odor complaints and mold problems are often due to poor maintenance of HVAC systems. The policy of a building manager might be, "We don't call someone unless there is a problem." It's best if large buildings have their own maintenance staff to take care of HVAC systems. Some buildings don't have dedicated maintenance staff, and outsource maintaining systems to HVAC contractors instead. These maintenance contracts are such that contractors are typically not looking for problems, they are just there to change the air filters.

Filters should be changed before they are visibly dirty. It's possible that dust collects outside on one corner of the building in such a way that while most of the air filters in the building may only need to be changed every three months, a few need to be changed monthly.

A common issue with air conditioning systems is the drip pan does not drain properly. A system may have been installed in such a way that the pan does not slope towards the drain or water may collect in the pan to the height of the drain pipe. Standing water supports bacteria growth and air rushing past standing water can be wicked, causing water to be splashed onto filters. If the filters get wet, mold can grow on them.

There is an ANSI standard on inspecting and maintaining HVAC systems, published by the American Society of Heating, Refrigeration and Air Conditioning Engineers (ASHRAE) and Air Conditioning Contractors of America (ACCA). If you hire a company to inspect the HVAC, ask to see their checklist. A visible inspection of the cooling coils and drip pan should be performed. It's rare, however, that an HVAC company will take the time to disassemble a system to the extent where a visible inspection of the cooling coils and drip pan is performed.

There is often some mold (yeast) growth on the cooling coils for HVAC systems, including those in drop ceilings inside what are referred to as "fan boxes." Cooling coils can be difficult to clean. Installing a UV light that shines directly on the coils can prevent yeast, bacteria, and mold growth on the surface of the coils, but the UV light must shine directly on the coils for it to work.

For some mold/odor investigations, the problem is a lack of fresh outdoor air. Ventilation with fresh outdoor air should be supplied to occupied spaces in accordance with the standard *ANSI/ASHRAE 62.1 Ventilation for Acceptable Indoor Air Quality.*

Commercial Buildings

Leadership in environment and energy design (LEED) recommends increasing outdoor ventilation rates 30% higher than what is recommended by ASHRAE 62.1. Increasing ventilation dilutes pollutants from personal and other sources. If an HVAC system is on the roof, it may have an inlet to pull in outdoor air. These are often closed to save money on heating and cooling, but they should always be kept open.

Remediation

The engineering controls to contain mold during remediation are similar to what is used for asbestos abatement. The most important step is to create a negative air pressure in the work area by using an air scrubber that is exhausted outdoors. The remediation company may complain about how difficult it is to exhaust the scrubber outside. A common excuse is how long the duct needs to be. Another is regarding security. These are just excuses for laziness or incompetence. Make sure you get what you pay for: containment with negative air pressure.

Never let a remediation company exhaust an air scrubber anywhere but outside. Some companies exhaust the scrubber into another occupied office space. They claim this is acceptable because they are using a HEPA filter. HEPA filters are only 99.9% effective. One-tenth of 1% might not sound a lot, but there can be trillions of spores in the air during remediation.

Do not allow the remediation company to use biocides or chemicals. You don't want tenants in the clean offices, those choosing to stay at work while remediation is performed, complaining about chemical odors.

Commercial Buildings

Keep the air clean. Chemicals do not remove mold. Cutting drywall out and sanding and cleaning wood remove mold. Everything else is a smoke and mirrors show to make you think the remediation workers are doing something more specialized. Building materials, especially porous ones, absorb odors from chemicals. These odors can cause headaches, poor concentration, and so forth. They can also create a headache for you, the building owner, when tenants complain. They are not needed, so don't allow them to be used.

Want to learn more?

Keeping Buildings Healthy, How to Monitor and Prevent Indoor Environmental Problems **by James O'Reilly, Philip Haga, Ronald Gots, and Alan Hedge (John Wiley & Sons, 1998) is an excellent resource for those managing or working in commercial buildings. In addition to mold, it covers lighting, noise, and other factors that influence perception about the indoor environmental quality in a building.**

ANSI/ASHRAE/ACCA Standard 180: Standard Practice for Inspection and Maintenance of Commercial Building HVAC Systems.

ANSI/ASHRAE Standard 62.1 Ventilation for Acceptable Indoor Air Quality.

Post-remediation
Verification

What to Do When the Mold Remediation Company Says They Are Finished

Step 1. Make sure the remediation company inspects their own work.

Although this sounds like common sense, it's often not done. Most of the time, the workers are day laborers who do what their boss tells them to and let the boss know when they are finished. The boss then calls the building owner and says the space is ready for testing without inspecting the work. The standard for professional mold remediation (S520) states it is the job of the remediation company to inspect their work before calling a mold inspector, as follows: "The evaluation performed by the remediation contractor shall include a visual inspection to ensure surfaces are clean and free of odors. The evaluation shall include moisture measurements to ensure surfaces are dry."

When the remediation company says an area is clean and ready for testing, they should shut off the air scrubbers 24 hours before telling you it is ready for testing. Some remediators scare clients into thinking the scrubbers must stay on until after the testing is done. This suggests they are not confident in their work. There was mold before they started and there wasn't an air scrubber. Why the sudden cause for concern? They are afraid that if they shut the air scrubbers off they will fail the air test. The air scrubber is a big air filter. Leaving it on during testing is not common sense.

Step 2. Inspect it

Everyone seems to want air samples, as if that's the best way to tell if the mold is gone. It's not. You can get good air sample results when there is still mold. Don't get distracted by the results of air tests; you want to be able to confidently conclude that all mold growth has been removed, which means the visual inspect is just as important as testing the air.

It's best to do a visual inspection yourself, before you call a mold inspector. The work area is frequently not as clean as the remediator claims it is, and you'd be wasting money calling a mold inspector before the space is fully cleaned.

If the air scrubber is still on (you will be able to hear it running), don't go inside the work area. Call the remediator and tell them to come and shut it off.

Once the air scrubber has been turned off for 24

hours, proceed. Wear Personal Protective Equipment (PPE) that includes a HEPA respirator. Start by peeking your head inside. If the floor looks dirty, call the remediator and tell them it needs to be re-cleaned.

If things look clean, notice how it smells. This is supposed to be the cleanest area in the building, so it should smell neutral. If you smell bleach or chemicals, don't go inside. A mold inspector cannot do a proper inspection until there are no chemical odors. If it smells musty or like mold, then there is likely still mold or a moisture problem that needs to be identified and removed. Ask the remediation company to figure it out. If they need assistance, get the mold inspector to help.

If the floor looks clean and the room smells neutral, keep going. Look for signs of mold, water damage, and dust. If you need to ask what you are looking for, that's a good sign. Look at the framing and sill plates. (Sill plates are the wood framing that run along the bottom of the floor.) Are there dark spots on the wood that look suspect? Is there rot? Rot needs to be cut out. If you see dust, smell mold, or see staining, it's not ready for testing. General contractors will tell you it's easier to cut out a sill plate and framing than to sand and clean. This is because cutting out materials is preferable to cleaning and improves the chances of passing the clearance test.

If a window leaked, mold is often hidden under the bottom of the windowsill. The only way to see and clean the mold is to remove the window. Ask the remediator to remove the window and the sill and rebuild the framing. Flash the window opening properly, then put a new window in without waiting to test the air. Don't rebuild the drywall on the interior side until the mold inspector has done an inspection and tested the air. While replacing the window, keep the door to the work area closed, and do as much of the work as possible from outside. It can help to staple plastic across the wall on the inside before removing the window from the outside. After the new window is in, remove the plastic and finish cleaning from the inside.

STEP 3. It's ready for testing

When the inspector arrives, they should do a visual inspection. If you've followed the steps so far, there shouldn't be any spots that look suspect. The mold inspector may also collect air samples. Leave the plastic containment in place until the laboratory results are satisfactory. If possible, leave the plastic and air scrubber in place during reconstruction to capture the dust generated during construction, keeping the occupants safe and happy.

Cleaning After Remediation is Finished

The following is a summary from *Dust Money: How to Clean Your Home and Belongings After Mold Remediation So You Don't Have to Throw Everything Away.*

Cleaning the HVAC System and Ductwork

If the HVAC ducts got wet, any ducts made with fibrous materials such as duct-board, fiberboard, or fiberglass should be removed and replaced. If the ducts and system did not get wet, then they are only dirty, and you may clean them. Duct cleaning is never 100% effective. It can be difficult to effectively clean ducts, especially flexible ducts. It's only practical to clean metal ducting. Flex-type ducting should be replaced.

Cleaning ducts is not a mold remediator's job. Hire a duct cleaning company for that. The ducts and the HVAC components should be cleaned prior to cleaning the house.

Cleaning Occupied Spaces

You have to empty a house before you can clean it. Put items in boxes and move the boxes outside or into a temporary storage. Inspect each item as you pack. Throw out items that have possible mold or smell like mold.

1. Prepare

Air-handling equipment (heating, ventilation, and air conditioning) should be shut down. Supply and return vents should be sealed with tape and plastic. If the ducts were cleaned, the air ducts and return registers should be sealed. Leave them sealed. Heavy furniture and furnishings that will not be removed should be wrapped with polyethylene sheeting. Carpet should be covered with plastic. Kitchen and bathroom cabinets that will not have the interiors cleaned or are not empty, should be covered with polyethylene sheeting and sealed.

2. Set up oscillating fans and an air scrubber

At least one oscillating fan should be aimed at each corner of each room. Place fans aimed up walls, at the ceiling, and so forth. The purpose is to minimize stagnant air zones where dust can settle.

An air scrubber should be placed in the middle of each room. If you have only one scrubber, consider placing it in the center of the house. In rooms without a scrubber, consider placing box fans in windows to blow air outside.

3. Air-wash

Turn on the fans and air scrubber. Walk through the house with a leaf blower, aiming it randomly. Direct the air to all corners of the rooms, ceiling, walls, tops of cabinets, steps, beams, doorjambs, light fixtures, and so forth.

4. Allow the dust to settle

Go outside and wait fifteen minutes, as that is approximately how long it will take for the dust to settle.

5. Vacuum

Go back inside and vacuum the floors. The purpose is to remove the bulk of the dust that blew out. Don't work too hard. Just get the big stuff.

6. Repeat

For the cleaning to be effective, it is important to use the leaf blower multiple times over the course of a day, with vacuuming in between.

Reposition the fans every two hours. Moving the fans ensures all parts of each room and the house get air movement, and minimizes dead zones.

7. Vacuum and damp wipe

Turn off and remove the fans and air scrubbers. Vacuum all surfaces (walls, top of cabinets, floors, and so forth). After vacuuming, use plain soap and water to damp wipe or mop all surfaces in the house. Use non-fragrant dish soap.

Cleaning Contents

There's no sense in cleaning the contents of a house if the house they're in is dirty. Proceed to clean contents only after the house has been cleaned. Items should have been packed into boxes and moved to a storage as the house was cleaned. Contents that had visible mold should have been discarded.

If something did not get wet, mold cannot grow on it. Clean these items as you would normally clean something dusty. Do not bother using bleach, chemicals, or biocides, as they won't help clean and may create new, objectionable odors and can be irritating. Use a leaf blower or compressed air hose to blow the dust off of them, vacuum them as thoroughly as possible, and wipe or wash them with plain soap and water. You can launder clothes with regular laundry soap. Take porous items like upholstered furniture or bedding outdoors and beat them with a stick while wearing a respirator and eye protection.

Cleaning After Remediation

The following spring cleaning tools are required:
- A bucket of water and fragrance-free dish soap
- A large quantity of rags
- Vacuum cleaner
- Leaf blower

Organize items into groups, based on type of material:
- Porous items (books, clothes, bedding)
- Semiporous items (wood furniture)
- Nonporous items (metal and glass)

Clean items outside. Anything that can be washed should be washed. Hard items such as plastic, metal, wood, and glass are easy to clean. Wipe these with soap and water or wash them. Clothes are also easy, just use regular laundry soap. Use a compressed air hose to clean the nooks and crannies of any item a vacuum cleaner or damp wipe cannot effectively clean. A computer is a good example of an item that benefits from the leaf blower or a compressed air hose. The compressed air hose or leaf blower should be used with caution, as it can break things and cause particles to fly that can damage your eyes. Always wear a respirator, goggles, and earplugs for protection.

The cleaning sequence is:

1. Wash item with soapy water. If an item can tolerate being submerged, wash the item.

Cleaning Contents

2. Air wash the item. This is the most important step for items that can't be washed. Blow these items with a compressed air hose or a leaf blower. This works well for books. Put a stack of books in a box, take the box outside, aim the leaf blower into it (while wearing goggles or a full-face respirator), and randomly flip pages and agitate the books. The leaf blower works well for boxes of knickknacks too. Place items in a clean box. Aim the blower into the box, taking care not to break or damage fragile items.

3. Vacuum the item. Although using a blower or compressed air hose is more effective than vacuuming, for some items, vacuuming is appropriate. An upholstered couch is a good example. I would use the blower on it after removing the cushions. Then I'd beat the cushions outside with a big stick.

4. Wipe the item. The last in the cleaning assembly is damp wiping. After using the blower to blow the bulk of the dust off, damp wipe the item with soap and water.

About the Author

Daniel Stih is an aerospace engineer and consultant who investigates homes and offices to solve complaints and health problems related to being indoors. He got started after retiring as an engineer and working as a handyman. After discovering that some of his clients were sick and were living in buildings that were making it difficult for them to become well again, he sought to help, researching testing and removal best practices to help them feel healthy again.

Photo by John Mate

Please visit www.healthylivingspaces.com.

If you are interested in learning how to do your own testing for mold, Daniel has a series of online courses. Go to www.academy.healthylivingspaces.com.

www.ingramcontent.com/pod-product-compliance
Lightning Source LLC
Chambersburg PA
CBHW070805100426
42742CB00012B/2259